WHO DO YOU THINK
YOU ARE ?

WHO DO YOU THINK YOU ARE?

Three Crucial Conversations for
Coaching Teens
to College and Career Success

Stephen M. Smith | Shaun Fanning

WILEY

Cover design: Paulina Maldonado

Published by John Wiley & Sons, Inc., Hoboken, New Jersey
Published simultaneously in Canada

For general information about our other products and services, please contact our Customer Care Department within the United States at (800) 762-2974, outside the United States at (317) 572-3993 or fax (317) 572-4002.

Wiley publishes in a variety of print and electronic formats and by print-on-demand. Some material included with standard print versions of this book may not be included in e-books or in print-on-demand. If this book refers to media such as a CD or DVD that is not included in the version you purchased, you may download this material at http://booksupport.wiley.com. For more information about Wiley products, visit www.wiley.com.

ISBN 9781119384700 (cloth)
ISBN 9781119384717 (ePub)
ISBN 9781119384748 (ePDF)

Printed in the United States of America

10 9 8 7 6 5 4 3 2 1

Contents

Contents

About the Authors

Shaun Fanning is chief product officer at Intellispark and a cofounder of Naviance. He previously served as vice president of research and development at Hobsons, where he led new product initiatives focused on improving student success through technology in K–12 and higher education. He joined Hobsons in 2007 through its acquisition of Naviance, where he served as head of product strategy and technology. Prior to cofounding Naviance, he held a variety of roles in business analysis, finance, technology, marketing, and product management at AT&T and The Thomson Corporation (now Thomson Reuters). He earned a BA degree in economics from Cornell University.

Stephen M. Smith is CEO of Intellispark, an education technology startup. He is vice chair of the board of College Possible, a member of the board of the National College Access Network, and a cofounder of Naviance. He previously served as president and chief product officer at Hobsons, where he led global product strategy, corporate development, student data privacy, and R&D. He joined Hobsons in 2007 through its acquisition of Naviance, where he served as chief executive officer. Prior to Naviance, he was vice president of digital product development at Peterson's, then a division of The Thomson Corporation (now Thomson Reuters). Prior to joining Peterson's, he was a founding member of the Internet consulting practice at Thomson Technology Services Group. He has also served as a practitioner faculty member at Johns Hopkins University and at Montgomery College. He earned a BA degree in history and an MBA, both from Cornell University.

Acknowledgments

We would like to thank the thousands of school counselors, teachers, administrators, and community mentors who trusted us, through Naviance, to join them in their journey to help transform the world through education. You inspired us, challenged us, and showed us every day how much of a difference a caring adult can make in the educational and personal trajectory of a child. We hope that through this book we can share many of the lessons we have learned from you and do our part to make the world a better place. We are lucky to have worked with you.

We are extremely grateful to Kim Oppelt for rounding out the book with her experience and knowledge in college admissions and financial aid—while remarkably also completing her doctoral dissertation and keeping up with the demands of a full-time job.

We appreciate the encouragement, insight, and feedback we received from Brandon Busteed, Laurie Cordova, Mary Docken, Patty Mason, and Nick Rabinovitch.

Thank you to Tom Zoldos, Paulina Maldonado, Lucian Slatineanu, and members of the Hobsons marketing team for your design, branding, and marketing support.

Thank you to Amy, Ruby, and Shepherd Fanning for giving up time with your dad and providing love and enthusiasm.

Last but not least, neither of us would be who we are today or have useful insights to share without our mothers, who believed without question in our wildest dreams, and our fathers, who taught us how to fight for those dreams.

Washington, DC
August 2017

PART

I

Who Are You?

1 | How Do You Get Started?

We are doing this all wrong. College gets more expensive and more competitive every year. Kids lose sleep over where they're applying and whether they'll be admitted. Parents are anxious and increasingly wonder whether college is a worthwhile investment. Those same parents ask a lot of important questions. *Will my child will get into a "good" college? How long will it take her to earn a degree? Can we afford tuition—not to mention room, board, and other expenses? Will she get a decent job after graduation? Will she be happy?* The problem, in most families anyway, is that we take the questions in the wrong order.

Brandon Busteed, the executive director of education and workforce development at Gallup, describes this process well. We start searching for colleges by thinking about attributes like size, selectivity, and location. We look into what majors are offered at the institution, and we may even consider sports programs or campus life. We probably look at the list price for tuition, room, board, and expenses, but because our system of education finance is so complex, those figures often bear little resemblance to what it will cost to attend. We build a list of colleges that meet our criteria. We visit some of those institutions to get a sense of how they "feel." We narrow the list and begin the arduous task of preparing and submitting college applications. By having focused our attention on list prices instead of the actual cost of attendance, we may have already ruled out some attractive options for financial reasons, even if those institutions may have turned out to be affordable. It's not until acceptances start coming in from colleges we chose to apply to that we get a better sense of the actual cost of attendance. For the vast majority of us, the cost of attending even an institution with a modest list price is higher than we can afford based solely on what we have saved or earn, so we explore loan options. After that, we decide where to enroll.

As many as half of all traditional-age first-year students enter college without declaring a major, and according to the National Center for Education Statistics (NCES) at the U.S. Department of Education, almost 80 percent change their major at least once after they enroll. So it's not until well after starting college and often taking on debt that families begin to understand how much the student will be likely to earn after graduation and what he can realistically afford to repay. Because such a high percentage of students change majors while in college, many are taking a long time to get to the finish line. In fact, NCES data show that only 44.2 percent of first-time bachelor's degree recipients earn a four-year degree in four years or less.

If you were designing this process from scratch, you might approach it from exactly the opposite direction. Start with the end in mind. Pick a career based on what you like to do. Research the labor market and find out how much you'll be likely be able to earn. Then look at the type of education required to get that job. Weigh the ability to pay for that education given your career prospects and reconsider if necessary. Once you're sure the cost of your education is manageable given your chosen career, enroll in the institution of your choice and complete your degree.

Many adult students (defined by the Department of Education as those age twenty-five and older) approach college in just this way. These students often enter college with specific career objectives. And although they're sometimes referred to as nontraditional or posttraditional students, this demographic now makes up the majority of college students in the United States. Can an approach that works for twenty-five-year-olds also help teenagers to make better college and career choices?

It's incredibly challenging for an adult to pick a major or a career, and developmental differences and comparatively limited life experiences make this decision even more overwhelming for teenagers. In that context, it's not surprising that so many college students change their minds after picking a major. Nonetheless, with poor retention and graduation rates at many colleges, few would argue that what we're doing now is working well. Something needs to change. By rethinking the path from middle and high school to college and career, we can reduce the stress and anxiety families feel and put more kids on track for a healthy and successful adult life.

This book got its start nearly seventeen years ago when we launched a program called Naviance and began working with high schools to improve how their students choose among colleges and universities. Since that time, more than 22 million kids around the world have researched college and career opportunities; selected middle and high school course work; gained important knowledge about what it means to go to college; and completed personality, strengths, and career interest assessments and other self-awareness activities in Naviance. These activities have helped those kids build a foundation for a thoughtful progression from school to college to work.

The goal of this book is to help more kids think about school and college with an objective in mind: recognizing that learning is intrinsically valuable and continues for life but that purposeful learning can be even more transformative. The question "Who do *you* think you are?" gets at the essence of what families need to explore to help their children make good college and career choices. The other questions posed throughout this book are meant to prompt crucial conversations that can help you and your teen, ideally with the support of your teen's school counselor, better inform the college and career search process.

Let's look at how the process typically works today. In U.S. elementary schools, there are few choices to make. Most kids in elementary school have a single teacher for all core academic subjects, even if there are separate faculty members for specialized courses in areas such as music, art, or physical education. While some subgroups of kids with particular needs, aptitudes, or interests might be selected to receive additional support, most follow a fairly consistent program and spend the majority of each day in the same room with the same teacher and the same classmates.

The environment is much different in secondary schools. By grade 6 or 7, schools frequently offer separate classes within core academic subjects for students who are performing at, above, or below grade level. Many schools have optional courses, known as electives, in subjects such as foreign language, instrumental music, and technology. Kids may still receive additional support if they need it, but they are also able to make many more choices to personalize their school experience. Many schools offer clubs and after-school sports. In grades 6 and 7, but especially by grade 8, the courses kids take have a direct impact on the courses they can take in high school, and as a result, their choices affect the majors they can select and even the colleges they may be able to attend.

Some of those connections are straightforward. For example, students who don't take algebra by the end of eighth grade typically can't complete the required course work to take calculus by twelfth grade, and those who don't take calculus before graduating from high school are at a significant disadvantage when applying to engineering and other quantitative programs in college. Other choices are a bit more complex since requirements for admission vary significantly from one college or university to another. Those requirements can even vary among schools and departments within the same college or university. The shared experiences in elementary school give way to a much more individualized program of studies and other activities in middle and high school, which can put kids on very different paths to life after earning a high school diploma.

How do you make sense of these choices? Is it even possible to ask a thirteen- or fourteen-year-old to think ahead ten years or more to consider how making a choice between taking algebra in eighth grade and choosing a slightly less demanding math class is likely to affect college or career options later in life? Is it possible to ask that same young person to weigh the benefits of taking another elective, and making time for the required homework, versus joining an additional after-school club? Choices like this one are being made by and for kids millions of times each year in U.S. schools, often with limited insight into the consequences. For some, it may even feel as though their plans are on autopilot. Those who have done well academically are often pushed to take every one of the most rigorous courses (regardless of their interest level in the subject) and to add even more to their plate through extracurricular activities based on their prior academic successes.

There's a false dichotomy playing out in many American schools. Kids with high grades get pushed to take more and harder courses, while those with lower grades are directed toward career-oriented programs. This approach sets up a tension between college and career. As one counselor in a highly regarded American high school told us, "At this school, college is the career." She conveyed that statement with no sense of irony or anxiety. For their four years in high school, every academic and extracurricular decision these students made at that school was intended to put them on a path to college. The purpose for which the high school was designed was to get its graduates admitted to a highly selective college or university with very little thought to what they might do once they earn a college degree.

This tension between college and career isn't unique to middle and high schools. On college campuses, too, it plays out on a regular basis. Some faculty, especially in the arts and humanities, bristle when earning a bachelor's degree is seen simply as a ticket to getting a job without an appropriate level of consideration for the intrinsic value of learning. One professor at an elite U.S. university explained, "My job is to teach English, not to get my students a job." Technically this professor is correct. His job is to teach English, and we share his love for the humanities. But nearly every one of his students will need to get a job after graduation—most of those outside academe—and there's nothing inconsistent or shameful about admitting that a degree in English is an outstanding qualification for many careers.

Because of this tension between college and career in schools and on college campuses, it can be difficult to have a constructive conversation about the role of academic preparation in developing the workforce. We don't mean to suggest that the subject doesn't come up. It does, both at cocktail parties and in policy circles. But too often college and career are presented as being at odds with one another. Kids in middle and high school are steered either to college *or* to the workforce. Courses in school or college are seen as either intellectual *or* vocational. College majors are presented as idealistic *or* practical. The truth is quite the opposite. Higher education is an important step on the path toward a better quality of life and a fulfilling career. And while some degrees are unquestionably more directly aligned with specific careers than others, the act of earning a four-year college degree is generally more important in enabling a stable, successful future than what or where kids study.

Nearly every career requires some form of preparation after high school: on-the-job training, a certificate, an associate degree, a bachelor's degree, or beyond. Research by the Georgetown University Center on Education and the Workforce (GUCEW) predicts that by 2020, 65 percent of all jobs will require some education or training beyond high school. A bachelor's degree, in particular, is a gateway to financial stability. A graduate from a four-year college or university will earn, on average, $1 million more than someone who finished high school but did not earn a four-year degree. We recognize that a four-year degree on its own is not a guarantee of future earnings and acknowledge that it's possible to find fulfillment in a career and financial success, if that's what you're after, without a college degree. But throughout this book, we assume that you and your teen are interested in both. The odds of finding a fulfilling career and making financial ends meet are far greater in the United States for those with a college education than for those without. In 2016, GUCEW found that 11.5 million of the 11.6 million jobs created after the Great Recession were filled by people with at least some college-level education.

This book seeks to put aside the unnecessary tension between college and career. With it, we aim to help families, counselors, and kids take a pragmatic approach to making choices about what to study and what to do. Our approach is grounded in several key beliefs:

- Everyone deserves to be able to go to college.
- Everyone deserves to have a fulfilling career.
- Everyone is entitled to have an honest and open conversation with a caring adult about which options are really on the table and which aren't.
- Every academic program is a form of career preparation.
- Learning is valuable both intrinsically and extrinsically.
- Idealism is admirable, but realism is critical.

We call this approach *connecting learning to life*. By helping kids to see how their goals in life relate to their time in school, we hope they will come to see school as personally beneficial. Instructors who work with adult learners are trained to show their students what's in it for them. They recognize that when people can apply what they're doing to something that matters to them, they'll pay attention. Primary and secondary schools don't usually work this way. Instead, we send our children to school and expect them to pay attention in class. The motivation for doing well in school is some combination of earning good grades and avoiding parental frustration. Unfortunately this just doesn't work very well for many students.

Each year, the Gallup Student Poll measures how kids feel about school. In recent years, the poll has surveyed about 900,000 public school students annually in grades 5 through 12. The results have been startling, and although the poll is based on responses from those who opt in rather than a scientific sample of the overall population, they have been remarkably consistent. The more time kids spend in school, the less engaged they are. In fact, student engagement dropped every year from grades 5 to 11 and ticked up only slightly in grade 12 as kids were about to finish high school. Age, peers, and other factors influence these results, but lack of engagement is also associated with a lack of perceived relevance. Students disengage when they don't know how something they're learning can help them accomplish something they find meaningful, which can have a negative impact on their academic performance and future prospects.

Connecting learning to life is about bridging college and career in a constructive way. It's about looking at college and career choices as closely related decisions. It's about making sure that kids and families make academic decisions and commitments with as much visibility as possible into career opportunities.

We realize that careers are ever-changing, and that today's kids are likely to have several careers during their lifetimes. We understand that middle and high school kids have limited experience on which to base long-term decisions. We know that some careers have very specific education requirements, while others are more accessible to generalists. But it's too easy today to see each stage of education solely as preparation for the next stage of education while encouraging kids who excel in school to do more solely for that reason.

We think it makes more sense for kids and their families to make decisions about the courses they take in middle school and high school with a view to what they're trying to accomplish in college *and* career. We believe this is the right approach—not because you're trying to limit your child's options, but because you're trying to create them.

This brings us to the three main questions for this book—the questions we want to equip you to help your teen answer:

- Who are you?
- Where are you heading?
- How will you get where you want to go?

We've broken these three larger questions down into a series of smaller ones. In part 1, we encourage you and your teen to have some deeper conversations about interests and strengths and about what work means to you. These foundational conversations are intended to set a shared under-standing between you and your teen.

From there we move on to part 2, which looks at some potential paths. We look at science, technology, engineering, and math (the STEM topics). We explore medicine and social work, the liberal arts, fine arts, entrepreneur-ship, criminal justice, and other options. As we do, we also consider the economic consequences of various paths. The goal of these conversations is to help identify multiple pathways that align with your child's interests and strengths while prompting a discussion about implications. For example, a computer science career may be more immediately rewarding economically than a career in the fine arts, and the education decisions and investments you choose to make need to take that into account.

Finally, in part 3, we help teens build a plan of attack. Armed with an honest personal assessment and a clear sense of what they have to gain or lose, we share some practical advice. We help you to help your kids think about internship opportunities so they can try out a career before they commit. We help you work with them to consider whether college is a good option. We challenge some of the conventional wisdom about how to choose a college and offer ways to go to college that make financial sense, even when choosing to pursue a career path that tends to offer lower salaries.

Throughout the book, we provide tools to help with these conversations. We present the good and bad, and we try to make sure to help you consider a realistic range of options rather than prescribe a one-size-fits-all solution. We recognize that not every option is right for every kid or family. We have also compiled a directory of additional resources at the end of the book that can serve as a quick reference or a chance to go deeper in areas of particular interest.

While we designed Naviance as a platform for middle and high school students working with school counselors to explore their options after high school, this book is meant to spark meaningful conversations between teenagers and their parents beyond the inevitable questions: "Where are you going to college? What are you going to study? What do you want to be?" You know your child better than anyone, and discerning a path to college and career success is among the most important activities you'll do together. We hope this book will inform your conversations so that you and your child can feel more confident and less stressed during this critical process.

Although the book is linear, the conversations don't need to be. We suggest that you start with part 1, but beyond that, feel free to jump around as you try to fit these conversations into the hectic schedules that many teens and families face. Chapters 4 to 14 are written to be useful even if they're read independently, and chapter 15 provides a short wrap up. Based on your teen's interests or strengths, you might decide some parts are less relevant. If you know, for example, that studying science or engineering is a poor fit, skip chapter 5. If he or she is already committed to a job in social work, psychology, or teaching, you might only read chapter 7 before moving on to part 3.

Our work with schools and families over the past twenty years has taught us that there is a critical link between college and career and that decisions about college and career should be approached in tandem in a way that's rigorous but not rigid. As much as teens and their families can do to improve the quality of college and career decisions, there's no magic bullet and the process won't ever be entirely scientific. But by knowing themselves, taking time to consider where they're heading, and building a plan, teens can vastly improve the odds that they will find a good match between their education and career goals.

2 | What Are Your Interests and Strengths?

It's an age-old debate: Should you pick a course of study based on what you love, or should you pick a course of study based on what you think will improve your career prospects? A quick online search will turn up more than 1 million articles and more than a few books that support one or the other view. But let's be honest: if there were a simple answer, the debate would have been over long ago. The truth is that for most of us, college and career success is about making trade-offs. Those trade-offs could be about timing—taking advantage of short-term opportunities that set you up for long-term success. Or they could be about economics—agreeing to accept lower potential earnings to work in a job you truly love.

To make those trade-offs wisely, we think it makes sense for you and your child to think about what she loves, what she's good at, and what work means to her. Understanding each of these in detail will help you find a pathway for college and career that makes sense for her. In this chapter, we start with helping you think about interests and strengths.

Assessing Interests

What do you like to do? It's a simple question, and we think it's a great place to start the conversation. Before we get to anything more formal, take a few minutes yourself and with your teen to think about what each of you likes to do. Ask yourself what you spend your time doing when you're not being required to do anything at all. Jot down the top five or six things that come to mind. For me (Steve), the list looks something like this:

- Traveling
- Working and playing with technology
- Speaking in public
- Researching topics in business and in education
- Trying new restaurants
- Singing as well as playing and listening to music

Since I'm in my mid-forties, I have had many years of life experience to help build this list. I've tried things that I haven't liked very much and others that I liked a lot. I spent a lot of time in school. I have worked for several companies and in many different roles. I have started and stopped various hobbies. Even so, these answers provide only limited career direction. They're helpful but definitely not sufficient to help me choose from thousands of different career opportunities. Teenagers have much more limited experience to draw on.

To help a teen whose exposure to various areas of interest has been limited and to help an adult dig deeper to potentially discover areas of previously unidentified interest, it can be helpful to complete a more formal assessment. The most widely used framework for assessing occupational interests comes from the work of psychologist John L. Holland, beginning in the 1950s. Responding to his own frustrations with the career assessments of the time, Holland spent more than forty years developing and refining his theory of career choice. Through his work, Holland identified six occupational themes:

- *Realistic:* Involving practical, hands-on problems and solutions
- *Investigative:* Working with ideas, research, and thought work
- *Artistic:* Using forms, designs, and patterns with freedom to create
- *Social:* Serving or interacting with people

- *Enterprising:* Launching and leading projects
- *Conventional:* Following standard operating procedures and attending to detail

These themes, sometimes referred to by the abbreviation RIASEC, describe the type of work one might expect to do in a particular job and can be used to match individuals with potential careers.

Several assessments have been developed to help identify compatible occupational themes. One of the most common instruments U.S. schools use to help kids determine their career interests is the O*NET Interest Profiler produced by the U.S. Department of Labor. It's available in paper form or for download, and it has been incorporated into many widely used online college and career planning tools. The assessment includes 180 items to which one responds "like," "dislike," or "?". Items include "build kitchen cabinets" and "record information from customers applying for charge accounts." Based on the responses, the assessment identifies one primary theme and two secondary themes, which are aligned to a database the Department of Labor maintains containing more than nine hundred occupations. Someone whose primary theme is *enterprising* might be inclined toward starting a business or working in an early-stage company, while someone whose primary theme is *investigative* might find a role as a researcher or analyst more appealing.

The O*NET Interest Profiler is broadly used, but it's just one of many tools available to assess occupational themes. There are many other categories of tools that look at characteristics such as strengths, personality type, and learning styles that can also be useful in developing a picture of what may help someone succeed in school and in a career.

It's worth noting that Holland's occupational themes aren't specific to any one field. They simply describe the type of work. *Realistic* jobs are found in hospitality and *investigative* jobs in finance. But industry can also be an important factor in selecting a career. To link an occupational theme to specific lines of work, career clusters can be helpful. Career clusters were developed with support from Advance CTE, an association of leaders in career and technical education. Each of the sixteen career clusters represents a group of occupations and industries that share common skills and knowledge:[1]

- Agriculture, Food, and Natural Resources
- Architecture and Construction
- Arts, A/V Technology, and Communications

- Business Management and Administration
- Education and Training
- Finance
- Government and Policy Administration
- Health Science
- Hospitality and Tourism
- Human Services
- Information Technology
- Law, Public Safety, Corrections, and Security
- Manufacturing
- Marketing
- Science, Technology, Engineering, and Mathematics
- Transportation, Distribution, and Logistics

As you're assessing interests, you can look at the combination of the occupational themes that you identify through the O*NET Interest Profiler or a similar assessment, as well as your preference for one or more career clusters. As a simple example, someone who has a strong preference for the artistic occupational theme and is passionate about working in education and training might look to be an art teacher in a school or an educator in a museum. The relationship between primary and secondary occupational themes can also lead in interesting directions. For example, someone whose primary theme is artistic but has enterprising and conventional as secondary themes and an interest in business management might consider combining those into a role with a small business that's focused on conservation work.

One challenge with the O*NET Interest Profiler is that it asks questions that may seem a bit odd or that may ask a young person to have an opinion on something that's he's never experienced. For example, asking a fourteen-year-old whether he likes to "build kitchen cabinets" can seem a bit strange. Other assessments with seemingly more age-appropriate questions are available and also align to Holland's RIASEC occupational themes. Even so, it's reasonable to ask whether any assessment completed in thirty to forty minutes can reveal meaningful insights on which to base life decisions. It's also reasonable to ask whether an assessment your teen completes will be meaningful enough to guide decisions that have long-term consequences.

Despite the occasional odd question, the O*NET Interest Profiler is highly regarded in research terms for both reliability (i.e., consistency) and validity (i.e., accuracy) as a measurement of Holland's occupational themes. Holland's occupational themes have also been shown to be stable over time for most people, meaning that an accurate measurement isn't likely to change much as we age. For this reason, the O*NET Interest Profiler is considered a good first step in evaluating career interests.

Like any other assessment, however, interpreting the results requires some judgment. We often hear from students in schools we work with that the assessment results they receive are "fairly accurate," but that doesn't mean they should be deterministic. When I was in tenth grade, I completed a career assessment similar to today's O*NET Interest Profiler. Because it was the mid-1980s, the test was done with paper and pencil, but otherwise the process was fairly similar to what most of today's students do by computer. I answered a series of questions, and after the assessment was scored, I received some guidance about my interests and a list of careers that might appeal to me. While I don't remember any of the others on the list, more than thirty years later I can still vividly recall the top recommendation: county clerk. My reaction was mostly confusion. I was thirteen or fourteen at the time, and I knew little about how local government worked. I had never met our county clerk, and I had no idea what the job entailed.

Unfortunately, that's where the lesson ended. We completed the assessment during a single English class and got the results a short while later. But we didn't learn much about how the results could guide us in a more thoughtful career search or how we should think about the specific career recommendations provided by the assessment. As a result, that lesson had little lasting impact on me other than providing a useful anecdote for conversations with school counselors about career planning and for this book. The good news is that career counseling practices in middle and high schools have advanced quite a bit since the mid-1980s, and you and your teen will probably find any school-based career assessment activity more meaningful than it was for me.

Whether done at school, with a private counselor, or in the home, we view an assessment like the O*NET Interest Profiler as the start of a process and the results it provides as the basis for further discussion and research. In that sense, it's more like a paper map than the turn-by-turn directions you get today from your smartphone.

Assessing Strengths

What comes to mind when someone asks you about your strengths? Do you think about skills or talents, such as the ability to write clearly or solve difficult math problems? Do you focus instead on positive attributes or personality traits, such as optimism or resilience? Maybe you think about a mix of these. For some, the response to being asked about strengths is to think immediately about weaknesses or blind spots.

Over the past thirty years, a wide range of research has been done in the field of strengths-based leadership. Academic researchers and leadership development firms have looked at the definition of strengths and how they influence academic and career performance. This research has looked at talents, experience, expertise, personality traits, and more. Taken together with interests and an understanding of what work means to you, strengths are a critical lens through which to consider college and career options.

Probably the easiest way to get started with strengths is to think about compliments that you get. Maybe a friend has appreciated your loyalty or an employer has thanked you for your attention to detail. If you have a hard time thinking about compliments, ask those who know you best to share what they think you do especially well. Their answers may surprise you, and depending on what they are, it might not be obvious right away how those strengths will help you in college or in a career. You may also find that what people tell you are your strengths don't line up well with what you've identified as your interests, at least at first.

While I was working on this chapter, I spoke with a colleague about her experience with strengths. She mentioned that people she works with often compliment her project management skills. She appreciated the positive feedback, of course, but she wasn't sure how to react. Managing projects wasn't something she enjoyed doing. But as she thought more about it, she considered what makes a good project manager. Although project management itself wasn't something she wanted to do as a career, she came to realize that many of the skills that led other people to compliment her as a project manager also made her successful in other areas. Project managers are good communicators. They're good at tracking detail, inspire their teams, solve problems well when they arise, and negotiate well. Each of these skills can serve her well in lots of potential careers, including her role doing research into potential new products. As her experience shows, it can be helpful to think broadly about strengths and consider the underlying skills that you can use to support many different academic and career paths.

Simply put, strengths are your best attributes. They are positive factors and describe things that you can do well. Among the leaders in studying strengths is

Gallup, which defines *strengths* as "the ability to consistently provide near-perfect performance in a specific activity." According to Gallup, strengths come from a combination of talents, knowledge, and skills. Gallup offers two assessments, StrengthsFinder and StrengthsExplorer, that can help you identify strengths. StrengthsFinder, designed for late teens and adults, has 180 items and takes thirty to forty minutes. StrengthsExplorer is meant for children between the ages of ten and fourteen and has seventy-six questions. It takes about fifteen minutes to complete. Both assessments are available for purchase online, and many schools and colleges also provide Gallup's strengths assessments to staff and students. If your child's school uses Naviance, the school can provide student access to StrengthsExplorer at no additional charge.

Gallup groups strengths into themes: ten for StrengthsExplorer and thirty-four for StrengthsFinder. For StrengthsExplorer, the themes are:[2]

- *Achieving:* Youths especially talented in the Achieving theme like to accomplish things and have a great deal of energy.
- *Caring:* Youths especially talented in the Caring theme enjoy helping others.
- *Competing:* Youths especially talented in the Competing theme enjoy measuring their performance against that of others and have a great desire to win.
- *Confidence:* Youths especially talented in the Confidence theme believe in themselves and their ability to be successful in their endeavors.
- *Dependability:* Youths especially talented in the Dependability theme keep their promises and show a high level of responsibility.
- *Discoverer:* Youths especially talented in the Discoverer theme tend to be very curious and like to ask "Why?" and "How?"
- *Future Thinker:* Youths especially talented in the Future Thinker theme tend to think about what's possible beyond the present time, even beyond their lifetime.
- *Organizer:* Youths especially talented in the Organizer theme are good at scheduling, planning, and organizing.
- *Presence:* Youths especially talented in the Presence theme like to tell stories and be at the center of attention.
- *Relating:* Youths especially talented in the Relating theme are good at establishing meaningful friendships and maintaining them.

When you complete StrengthsExplorer, the assessment results list your top three themes. For StrengthsFinder, the results generally include your top five themes, although you can also choose to see how strongly your results indicate each of the other themes.

Strengths versus Weaknesses

At the beginning of the chapter, we asked what comes to mind when you think about your strengths. For some, it's hard to think about strengths without also considering weaknesses. In fact, many people spend more time thinking about weaknesses than strengths, believing that improving on weaknesses is the optimal path to self-improvement.

Gallup's research found that this focus on weaknesses spans cultures, age groups, and levels of education: "Whether we asked the question of the American population, the British, the French, the Canadian, the Japanese, or the Chinese, whether the people were young or old, rich or poor, highly educated or less so, the answer was always the same: weaknesses, not strengths, deserve the most attention."[3] Most people, it seems, worry more about fixing their weaknesses than building on their strengths. Research by Gallup and others suggests this is a mistake. It's not that weaknesses should be ignored, but, on balance, you are likely to have greater success by building from a position of strength than by trying to compensate for an area of weakness.

Zenger Folkman, a leadership development consultancy, has looked at the qualities that allow some leaders to stand out among their peers. Their research is based on more than 850,000 assessments conducted of leaders by peers and subordinates. In *Key Insights from the Extraordinary Leader,* Zenger Folkman found that "the key to developing great leadership is to build strengths."[4] Yet they noted that the executives with whom they work consistently "ignore the pages describing their strengths, and immediately focus on the weaknesses."[5] This instinct to focus on weaknesses comes with an opportunity cost: a reduced focus on building strengths, which is problematic since "the more strengths people have, the more likely they are to be perceived as great leaders."[6]

It's not that weaknesses should be ignored. Some weaknesses are so limiting that they can inhibit strengths. In other cases, weaknesses can get in the way of your interests. For example, if you're interested in a career in engineering but struggle with math, you'll need to work to overcome that weakness to achieve success. The best advice we can offer is to look for opportunities where your interests and strengths align and build from there.

Using Interests and Strengths When Exploring Colleges and Careers

Knowing what I do now about how to explore careers, if I could go back to that day in tenth grade English when I was advised to be a county clerk or if I were sitting with a teenager today, I would still use an assessment to think about interests, and I'd also include a separate assessment of strengths, but would approach the entire lesson a little differently:

1. *Establish context.* Before your teen takes any assessment, talk with her about the various factors that can influence a successful career choice. Explain that interests and strengths are useful lenses through which to consider career options, but that timing, financial realities, and other issues also play a role.
2. *Set expectations.* Discuss the assessment that you're using. If you plan to use the O*NET Interest Profiler, acknowledge that some of the language may be unfamiliar but encourage your teen to look past it while focusing on the benefit of the assessment results. It may be helpful to explain the research that went into it to encourage her to take the process seriously.
3. *Think expansively.* Most of us are guilty of going straight to the last page of an exam or research paper to see the grade while skipping past any comments the teacher provided, yet the comments are often extremely helpful. The same is true of career assessment results. Instead of focusing on a specific list of jobs, encourage your teen to read and consider any comments about the results and think broadly about any specific careers and what direction those may provide as she considers all of her options.
4. *Start a conversation.* Don't let the assessment result be an end in itself. The career assessment that recommended a career as a county clerk for me could have been a solid basis for a discussion about what a county clerk does, whether that might be appealing to me, and whether any of those responsibilities would be good qualifications for other jobs. Unfortunately, the results didn't prompt any discussion, and the activity was a waste of time.

Are Careers Inherited?

When we're talking about career exploration with teens, one of the greatest challenges is their limited personal experience. As research has shown, other family members' career choices can be hugely influential, as can the examples of other community role models.

Facebook's data science team has done some interesting work in this area. Using the massive amount of data that Facebook generates about its members, researchers looked at how parental and sibling careers influence other family members' career choices. Two of the data scientists who worked on the project shared their findings in an article, "Do Jobs Run in Families?"[7] They found that for many occupations, there is a relationship between parents' careers and the careers their kids chose. Similarly, there is a relationship among siblings' career choices, which is even stronger among twins. The authors note, for example, that sons whose fathers serve in the military are five times more likely to enter the military than other men and that daughters whose fathers worked as scientists were 3.9 times as likely to choose to work as scientists themselves.

The article is careful to note that despite the striking examples they provide, many more children strike out on their own than follow in the footsteps of their parents and siblings. It also doesn't attempt to demonstrate the cause for the relationships, which can also be heavily influenced by factors such as education level, socioeconomic status, and gender, among others, that correlate with job choices.

So while parents' and siblings' career choices influence other family members, the choices made by others in the community and the availability of role models are also important. These effects can be extreme in communities with high levels of poverty and unemployment, where the examples of various career paths are often limited. But these effects can also be meaningful in rural areas or other communities where young people don't have exposure to many different career paths. Not surprisingly, it's hard for kids to envision themselves doing jobs that they don't know exist. For this reason, we encourage you to help your teen cast a wide net and explore opportunities that may not be immediately obvious.

Future-Proofing Career Choices

One of the reasons that we encourage you to treat a career interest assessment as one element of a broader career research effort is that job opportunities change dramatically over time.

The U.S. Department of Labor has estimated that 65 percent of today's elementary school students will work in careers that don't yet exist. Consider that as this book is being published in 2017, many of the technologies that we now take for granted are younger than the teens we're coaching. Google has existed for fewer than twenty years, and Facebook has been around for just thirteen. Apple will celebrate the tenth anniversary of its iPhone this year, and the App Store that enabled so many of the new capabilities that we now associate with smartphones came even later. Today, job listings for mobile application developers, data scientists, and social media managers are plentiful. These roles didn't exist when I completed my career assessment in high school.

A risk of taking recommended jobs too literally is that you prepare for the present at the expense of the future. The Department of Labor does an impressive job categorizing and updating the more than nine hundred occupations in its database, but with 125 million people employed full-time in the United States the level of variety is far greater than the list can capture, and new jobs are being created every day.

Even as the pace of change in careers accelerates, the research around interests has nevertheless remained remarkably stable for more than fifty years and provides a good basis from which to discuss the types of work that your teen might be best suited to do.

Connecting Your Interests and Strengths to High School Courses

So how does this focus on interests and strengths affect your high school course work? It's unlikely that you'll find listings in your high school course catalogue mapped to Holland's RIASEC or Gallup's strengths themes. It is, however, increasingly common in course catalogues to find references to career clusters and defined career pathways, which can be a great place to start. In some middle and high schools, some form of strengths assessment is part of the curriculum for students and a regular professional development activity for teachers, which helps to create a common vocabulary to discuss future opportunities.

Balancing the Ups and Downs

Coming back to the question that kicked off this chapter, should you choose your course work and career path based on what you love to do or extrinsic factors such as employment prospects and income? It's really a trick question since you need to balance both. Even as you try to apply your interests and strengths to developing a career pathway, financial realities may limit your flexibility. And even if you're lucky enough to find a job in a field that you love, great jobs come with ups and downs.

Many books encourage their readers to find a passion and stick with it. We tend to be a bit more pragmatic. Use each step in your education and career to move closer to your ideal combination of interests and strengths while considering for your financial needs.

3

What Does Work Mean to You?

Like many kids, I (Steve) grew up without knowing that much about our family's finances. I knew that my dad had to work so that we could afford to live, and I knew that my mom chose to work so that we could have a little extra money for discretionary expenses. I knew some families had more than we did and that some families had less. But in the small, middle-class town where I grew up, the range I experienced was narrow. I didn't know any families that were extremely wealthy or extremely poor, and it was taken as a given that people worked so that they could support their families.

When I got to college, I saw that some of my classmates lived very differently from me. Some were very rich. They drove amazing cars and took exotic vacations with their family and friends. Others were very poor and had almost no money beyond the financial aid they received to enable them to pay tuition. It wasn't until I saw these extremes that I started to understand that work could mean really different things to different people.

For some of my wealthiest classmates, work was optional. Some counted on the jobs they hoped to get after graduation for status more so than money. Others weren't interested in either status or money and instead looked for

meaning or opted to do very little. For those with more limited means, the
job after graduation was a critical step on the economic ladder. While they
hoped to find meaning in their work, they needed a salary to pay back student
loans and ensure their time in college was a good investment, and that took
precedence over the type of work.

Over more than twenty years of working on issues of college and career
readiness, I've known many college advisors who try to avoid the topic of
money, a topic that is both very personal and very complex. It's tempting to
say that college and university choices should not be made on the basis of
money. While it's true that a small number of well-funded institutions pledge
to be need blind in admissions and that a smaller number commit to meeting
the financial needs of any student who is admitted, most colleges and
universities don't have the resources to make these commitments. And
even institutions that are need blind and commit to meeting students'
financial needs use funding formulas that may not calculate need in the
same way a family or student does. As a result, for all but the most affluent
students or those admitted to the wealthiest institutions, money is a consideration in the choice of where to attend college.

It's an awkward topic, but money is at the heart of the question of
what work means to you. If your family has a lot of it, you have flexibility.
Family financial support could allow your teen to make college and career
choices solely based on interests and strengths. Most of us don't have that
luxury, though. Even if we are lucky enough to find personal fulfillment
at work, our career choice (and the education decisions we make to
support it) has to support our lifestyle. We need to earn enough each year
to pay rent or a mortgage, plan for our own kids' education, and save for
retirement.

Having the Tough Conversation

Given the role money plays in college and career options, we believe it's
critical that you and your teen address the topic head-on and use it as a
foundation for a broader discussion about the meaning of work. Going to
college or university is expensive: the cost of tuition, room, board, books,
expenses, and for many students, the added cost of earning little or no salary
while they're in school. We say more about financial aid in chapter 12, but

even if your family qualifies for financial aid, you may still be expected to make contributions that stretch your budget.

As much as we might wish the opposite, financial realities play a significant role in determining what college and career choices are realistic. Many of my more affluent college classmates could afford to take time off after graduation or take a job with a comparatively low salary because they didn't face the same financial pressures I did to cover my own cost of living. My less affluent classmates had even greater pressures than I did since they had not only the cost of living after graduation but the cost of repaying loans.

I enrolled in college in the late 1980s. At the time tuition, room, and board at a four-year public university totaled just over $4,600 per year, while those costs averaged more than $13,000 annually at a four-year private university. I had almost no idea what my parents made or what it cost them to provide a home for my brother and me. The most I'd ever earned in a year was a few thousand dollars from a couple of part-time jobs. Although my parents were extremely generous and offered to cover the cost of my undergraduate education, I had no way of knowing what, if any, financial pressure my college choices would put on my family.

Shortly after I enrolled in university, I decided to change my major, which meant transferring to a different college within the university and nearly tripling my tuition. This decision caused tremendous stress for my parents. A lot of that stress came because they worried that my new major, history, would limit my employment prospects (more on that in chapter 5). But another important source of stress was cost. As a seventeen-year-old college student who had never made a major purchase in my life and who knew little about my parents' financial situation, the impact of my decision wasn't clear to me. In fact, it never occurred to me that my decision to change majors could upend the financial plans my parents had carefully made over several years. To make it work, they took out a home equity line of credit even as they faced the prospect of paying tuition for my younger brother just two years later, something I didn't know at the time and probably wouldn't have understood because we rarely talked about money.

As you and your teen think about college and career decisions, it's important to consider your finances and what work means to you—and to be transparent with one another. Your children can't understand the economic realities of their choices on their own. With the benefit of hindsight, my family could have avoided a lot of anxiety and focused on realistic options if we had tackled these issues long before I ever built my college list and submitted my applications. Here are a few questions we think it's important to ask and answer right up front:

- *Who will pay for college and for how long?* There's no right answer to this question. In some families, parents or grandparents pay for college. In other families, parents or grandparents contribute a portion of the overall cost. In my case, my parents agreed to pay for four years of undergraduate studies. I knew going in that I needed to finish in four years or I'd have to find a way to pay for the remaining time. I also knew when I started college that if and when I decided to get a master's degree, I'd pay for that on my own. This was useful in helping me to think about what I would do when I graduated.
- *How much have you saved for college?* Qualified tuition plans, commonly called 529 plans, can be a great way for families to save for college, and they provide some tax advantages. Beyond that, kids and families can also save money in traditional savings and investment accounts. But before your teen chooses a college, have a conversation about how much you've collectively saved.
- *Will your teen work during college?* According to a report from the Georgetown University Center on Education and the Workforce, more than 70 percent of college students work while in school.[1] If your teen will be working, be sure to discuss what portion of those earnings will be used toward college tuition.
- *What can the family afford to spend on college?* After you consider savings, discuss how much of the family's income can realistically be spent on college expenses each year. Be sure to plan ahead as any other children in the family approach college age. In the end, only you can decide what is affordable for your family.
- *If there's a gap, what options are available, and who will pay?* Are you or another adult willing to cosign loans on behalf of your teen? Is your child likely to qualify for merit-based funding, such as academic or athletic scholarships?
- *Do you have a contingency plan?* Discuss how you'll handle changes to your plan. Consider the effects of losing a job or a serious family illness or the inevitable annual increase in the overall comprehensive cost of the college. Data from the U.S. Department of Education suggest that 80 percent of students change majors at least once on their way to a bachelor's degree, so discuss how you would react if your teen wants to change majors or transfer to another institution.

- *Where do you expect your child to live after graduation, and who will pay expenses?* My dad was very clear that I could live at home, at no cost, for up to six months after graduation. Beyond six months, I was expected to find my own place to live at my own expense.

After you have a clear picture of the family's available resources, you are ready to take the next step and help your teen understand what it costs to live.

Setting Expectations

A couple of years ago, I had an opportunity to speak with a group of students at a local high school about their plans after senior year. Graduation was coming, and nearly all were heading to college in the fall. They were excited and looking forward to the next step in their lives.

The conversation moved through many different topics, but I found the discussion about life after college especially interesting. In fact, it was a generation-defining experience for me.

When I was growing up, my parents would, in good humor, often remind me how much easier my life was than theirs had been at my age. I had my own room, while they had to share. The school bus picked me up just outside our front door, while they walked to school—uphill both ways, my dad used to say, to amplify the point. (I mostly rolled my eyes as any good teenager would.) What they were hoping I would learn was that I was pretty lucky and that I should not take my situation for granted. Someone, in this case the two of them, made it possible for me to grow up mostly shielded from the realities of making a living and making difficult trade-offs.

On that day, in that classroom with those seniors who were approaching graduation, I saw myself as a teenager and learned a new appreciation for the challenge parents face in teaching their kids about how to make their own way in the world. As we talked, it became clear that these sixteen- and seventeen-year-olds started with the assumption that the physical comforts that their parents provided were the baseline. Even as they went off to college and ultimately started out on their own, they expected to have at age twenty-one or twenty-two what their parents could now afford. These teenagers had a limited understanding of what they could reasonably expect to earn after graduation from college and an even more limited understanding of what life costs. Even if they understood the idea of a mortgage or monthly rent, they often didn't have a clear picture of the amount, and they didn't have a full appreciation for the other costs they'd incur: taxes, food, utilities, insurance, gasoline. Most assumed that things would just "work out" or that their parents would make up the difference, not surprising since a recent survey found that a third of U.S. households provide financial support to adult children.[2]

Before committing to college and career decisions, it's important to take time to set expectations for what life will look like after graduation. Just as you should agree to the financial parameters that define college costs, you and your teen should lay out a financial plan for graduation and beyond.

We suggest the following:

- *Build a postgraduation budget.* Give some thought to where and how your teen might want to live—for example, urban, suburban, or rural location; type and quality of housing; solo or with a roommate. Estimate costs for rent and other expenses, including taxes, food, utilities, insurance, and any costs of commuting to work. If you expect your teen to have to repay college loans, be sure to estimate the monthly payments.
- *Based on income needs and on interests and strengths, make a list of careers.* Many career search tools, including the U.S. Department of Labor's CareerOneStop (https://www.careeronestop.org) from the U.S. Department of Labor, allow you to search salary and wage information for various careers. These data can help you find jobs that align with interests, strengths, and financial needs.
- *Research college costs.* The U.S. Department of Education compiles apples-to-apples data on tuition, fees, room, board, and expenses for colleges and universities throughout the United States. You can find the most recent information at CollegeNavigator.gov and on many other college search websites. The actual costs may vary dramatically based on family income and other factors, however, so you'll want to look at the net price in addition to the list price. Read chapter 12 on financial aid in this book for more information. Compare these costs to what your family can afford to spend and to what you've included in your postgraduation budget.
- *If there's a mismatch, start over.* Ideally you will have found a great match that aligns interests, needs, and financial realities, but if not, it's better to address that issue early. Later in the book we'll look at some alternatives, including 2 + 2 programs that allow students to start earning a bachelor's degree in community college, where tuition and fees are much lower, before transferring to a state university to complete the final two years.

The process of building a postgraduation budget is an opportunity to bring transparency to future financial discussions, and it serves as a foundation for discussing career and college decisions. By helping your teen understand the cost implications of different living arrangements, you can prompt a discussion about the trade-offs he or she is willing to make. Sharing an apartment that's a short distance outside the city center can save a lot of money and increase flexibility when choosing a career or selecting a college. Living at home for a time after graduation, if it works for all family members, can make it much easier for a recent college graduate to accelerate loan payments or build savings. Conversely, high-cost living arrangements can be overwhelming for many young people early in their careers in almost any field.

What Role Does Work Play in Your Life?

Much of this chapter has focused on money, so much so that I'm worried you might think I'm putting too much emphasis on maximizing earnings. We started with money only because it drives a lot of the discussion. With money comes greater flexibility for both career and college choices. And if the choices you make are not aligned, you can find yourself struggling to meet your basic obligations. But once you've figured out the financial realities and understand the minimum that you'll need to support your career and college decisions, it's crucial to look at the broader role that work plays in your life. This is where profit meets purpose.

As an undergraduate, I knew I needed a job after graduation. To move out on my own within the six-month time frame my dad set for me, I had no choice. With the need to pay my own rent and buy my own food, my first job was mainly about economics. For my first job after college, I worked as a technical writer. It wasn't glamorous work, but it could have been a lot worse. I got early access to new computer software, which appealed to the tech geek in me, but writing detailed instructions for word processing and database applications got a bit tedious over time. As a twenty-one-year-old recent college graduate, however, the job fit into my life quite well. I enjoyed my coworkers, I got some good experience to put on my résumé. And I was able to pay my rent while putting away a little money in savings.

After a couple of years, I took another look at the role that work played in my life. Having saved a little money and proved to my parents that I was employable despite my liberal arts education (more on that in chapter 5), I decided to pursue an MBA. By complementing my liberal arts degree with some formal training in business, I figured that I could make myself even more valuable to a future employer. Enrolling in business school immediately after earning my bachelor's degree had not been an option for me. My parents and I had agreed that I needed to pay for any graduate studies, and I didn't have the money to stay in school. But the decisions I made that got me to my first job provided some flexibility, which I exercised when I went to business school.

Truth be told, I wasn't the classic MBA student. I completed my core courses but took about as many non–business school courses as I could that would still count toward my MBA—including courses in music and history that I wished I'd had time to take as an undergraduate. What business school became for me, however, was an opportunity to find meaning in work.

I finished my MBA in 1995, well before tech start-ups captured everyone's imagination. In fact, the entrepreneurship program at my business school at the time consisted of a single course, which, as it turns out, is one of just two courses I took in business school that I still apply in my work nearly every day. The clear expectation for a "good" business school student at the time was to do well in school and then find a job with a big company. But that didn't appeal to me.

While many of my classmates found internships between their first and second years of business school with companies like Goldman Sachs, Procter & Gamble, and Pfizer (names that would have made my parents very happy), I decided to stay on campus that summer. I got a part-time job in a research lab at Cornell's College of Engineering called, creatively enough, the Engineering Multimedia Research Lab (EMRL). While an internship at any of the firms I mentioned would have given me worthwhile business experience, I decided I wanted to go a bit deeper in technology, something the EMRL was well suited to do. The year was 1994, and the Netscape web browser would be introduced that fall. While my friends and classmates were building spreadsheet models in their internships, I had an opportunity to work with a prerelease version of Netscape and begin experimenting with what would come to be called the World Wide Web before most people had even heard of it. As we started to see how easy it would be to share information through a simple online interface, those of us working in the EMRL got very excited. Our mission that summer was to explore ways to improve undergraduate engineering education, but we could see immediately that the potential applications spanned education and virtually every industry.

Although working in the EMRL was my job, it also sparked a greater interest for me in technology and convinced me that I wanted to start my own technology business. While working in the EMRL, I met Shaun, with whom eight years later I would cofound Naviance and sixteen years after that would coauthor this book.

When I finished my MBA in 1995, starting a business simply wasn't in the cards. The role that work played at that point in my life was to repay my student loans. My newly minted MBA, combined with my EMRL experience, did help me find a good job working as a technology project manager for the Thomson Corporation (now Thomson Reuters). In that role, I worked with a variety of Thomson-owned companies, one of which, Peterson's, published education directories. I did a couple of projects with Peterson's before being offered a full-time opportunity. By 1999, I'd convinced Shaun to join me at Peterson's, and we worked on an intrapreneurship project to launch a new college-search website. By 2001, the two of us had saved some money and were ready to take more risk. In 2002, we launched Naviance—an online tool that millions of students use to make career and college decisions—which gave us an opportunity to combine our interests and our strengths in an entrepreneurial venture and allowed us to find an even greater sense of meaning in our work.

Finding Meaning

We hope that everyone can find meaning at some point in their career work that provides intrinsic value rather than just extrinsic reward. But the reality is that meaning comes in different forms at different times. As I've tried to illustrate with the story of my own career development, the process of understanding interests, strengths, and meaning in work provides a long-term direction, but it doesn't mean ignoring current realities.

Many of the students we've worked with need to make career decisions based on short-term needs. With the pressures of meeting living expenses and repaying student loans, compromises between what you'd most like to do and what you can afford to do at a particular point in time are inevitable. That's not an argument against understanding interests and strengths or a reason to abandon your quest to maximize meaning in your work. Instead, we think it's an argument for calling out the search for meaning in your work and making that an explicit part of your long-term plan.

Those who study workplace performance are particularly focused on measuring engagement, which is the level of emotional commitment employees bring to their work. Engagement is a good proxy for the meaning that employees derive from their jobs, and it's strongly associated with higher levels of performance. Unfortunately, employee engagement is pretty rare in the United States. According to Gallup, nearly 70 percent of U.S. workers are not engaged at work, which costs the national economy between $483 billion and $605 billion per year.[3] The benefits to employers are considerable. Companies with highly engaged employees enjoy higher performance and lower costs than those with less engaged staff. But there are substantial benefits for employees as well, reflected in lower rates of turnover, fewer work-related injuries, better-quality work, and higher levels of productivity.

One way to think about your level of engagement at work is to ask yourself whether you view work as a job, a career, or a calling. Professor Amy Wrzesniewski at Yale University's School of Management identified these three categories in her research on employees' perceptions of their jobs. Although higher levels of engagement can be correlated with certain types of jobs and workplace seniority, those correlations are not absolute. The differences among a job, a career, and a calling are about mind-set.

The well-known story of three bricklayers is one of my favorite ways to illustrate the power of finding meaning at work. When asked what they were doing, the first of the bricklayers answers flatly, "I am laying bricks." The second, with a greater sense of awareness of his work, answers, "I am building a wall." The third, with a full appreciation of the purpose of his work and a clear sense of meaning, said, "I am creating a cathedral that will stand for generations." Each of these individuals had an identical job. Each earned identical wages. Only their perspectives differed.

The story of the bricklayers helps to show that it's possible to find meaning even in a job that can feel repetitive or mundane. In my own career, the knowledge that I had a plan—not turn-by-turn directions, but a general sense of direction—helped me to find meaning at each stage even as I made the short-term trade-offs that were necessary. At points where that sense of meaning started to fade, I knew it was time for a change.

PART II

Where Are You Heading?

4

Are You Ready for a Career in Science, Technology, Engineering, or Math?

Just before I (Shaun) sat down to start this chapter, NASA announced the discovery of a nearby solar system with seven planets that are close to the size of Earth, all of which could have water and temperatures that are suitable for life. I watched a live video feed as researchers explained with excitement the painstaking scientific process behind their inspiring find. It was a beautiful mix of astrophysics, mathematical deduction, and clever software engineering to repurpose a space probe that wasn't even designed to look for planets. As the story unfolded, I couldn't help but feel a wave of emotion because science was the first subject in school that sparked a true passion in me, and that passion led me to start college as a physics major, bent on unlocking some secret of the universe with an almost religious zeal.

My life and career since that time have strayed far from that earnest dream. A Nobel Prize or even just the deep satisfaction of revealing a small piece of nature's inner workings will never be a part of my story. Things have worked out just fine for me, but studying science in college was nothing like I expected, and the realities of a career in science, technology, engineering, or math (STEM) do not always line up with the recruiting pitch that promises that going into a STEM career will help you change the world. The world of STEM careers is a vast topic, which is part of its appeal, but we focus in this chapter on how to think about STEM careers in a more general sense, how to ensure your child is prepared for a STEM education and how to help your child determine if STEM is a promising pathway or a mismatch between reality and expectations.

STEM Pathways

Many people assume that a STEM degree will make it easy to find a high-paying job after college because there is a shortage of qualified graduates entering most scientific and engineering fields. The truth is that for many scientific, technology, and engineering jobs, there are plenty of qualified candidates, and the most desirable and high-paying jobs are highly competitive. This doesn't mean that a STEM degree is a bad idea. In fact, a STEM degree is statistically more likely to result in higher starting salaries out of college and higher earnings on average than many other areas of study. But the details matter. There are some big differences in job prospects and earning potential depending on one's specific career interests, and students should give some thought to these differences as they plan their education and career. Let's look, for example, at the difference between what I'll call a scientific pathway and a technical pathway.

If I said that someday I wanted to be an astrophysicist, a marine biologist, or a genetic researcher, I would generally be on a more scientific pathway. A scientific pathway typically begins in college with a four-year undergraduate degree in core fields like physics, biology, or mathematics and most often then requires extensive postgraduate education such as a master's degree, a doctorate, and then a postdoctoral fellowship where I would participate in research and be mentored until I could find longer-term employment in my field. If I were truly driven by furthering scientific research, my employment after my postdoc would then typically be with a research institute, a project funded by a large grant or a teaching position with a college or university that may or may not include a requirement on my part to continue advancing my field and getting my work published on a regular basis. I might be doing fundamental research on the big bang theory or studying what makes our cells age and our bodies grow old. The best of these jobs at the best of these institutions are extremely competitive. These are literally the smartest people in the world. In this pathway, it would be quite common for me to be in my late twenties or early thirties before I found sustainable long-term employment and was earning a decent salary to support a family.

These are truly some of the most important, interesting, and meaningful careers in the world today. This is the type of career that inspired me to work hard in high school and achieve admission to one of the world's top scientific research universities. To this day, I admire with longing the scientists who make mind-blowing discoveries and advance human knowledge. But students need to have their eyes wide open going into such a path because it can take a long time to achieve the kind of career stability, financial well-being, and work-life balance that their peers may achieve much earlier in other career fields. In addition, the federal government has substantially reduced funding levels for pure scientific research over the past several years and with the current administration, this trend may accelerate dramatically. Unfortunately this has directly reduced research opportunities, and therefore employment prospects, for those with advanced STEM degrees. In fact, I have observed a common pattern among friends and colleagues who earned an advanced scientific degree in a subject like math or physics. They jumped from the research world into the corporate world with a well-paying role in which they could leverage some of their scientific expertise and mathematical skill to solve business problems such as designing products (e.g., self-driving cars) or increasing sales (e.g., statistical analysis of the most effective marketing channels).

In contrast to the scientific path, the technical path is about obtaining technical skills that can be immediately useful to employers that need to solve practical problems. These are careers like making robots that manufacture microchips, programming computers to track financial transactions, designing car engines, or building a mobile phone app like Instagram. Parents tend to like the idea of these careers for their children because they perceive that there are plenty of interesting and well-paying jobs waiting for students with these kinds of degrees. In a broad sense, this is true. On average, a student graduating with a degree in electrical engineering will be a lot more likely to find a well-paying job than a student graduating with a degree in philosophy. But it's important for students to understand that a technical path does not come with a guarantee that the work will pay well or be fascinating.

Entry-level technical jobs at top companies are highly competitive, and that means that companies will be looking for students with excellent grades and may prefer students who have already interned with them during summers.

Getting admitted to a good engineering or technical program in college is just the first step and in some ways the easiest. These are demanding degrees with intense mathematical course work and a lot of project-based learning that requires teamwork, open-ended problem solving, and self-discipline. The engineers designing self-driving cars are the ones who made it through that gauntlet with flying colors. The good news, which I discuss more later in this chapter, is that a STEM degree is also great preparation for careers outside scientific and technical fields as well, so even students who realize they are not cut out to be hard-core technical engineers and are not at the top of their graduating class are still well prepared to find a good career in many areas that are growing and paying above average.

A common assumption about STEM is that you need a STEM degree to pursue a STEM career. This may be true with a field like nuclear physics or biomechanical engineering, but there are now many ways to enter a field like software engineering or information technology without a formal STEM degree. The world of computer technology, in particular, has a long tradition of successful members who were self-taught or transitioned unexpectedly from careers such as a jazz musician, history PhD candidate, and even the unfairly maligned philosophy major. "Coding boot camps" allow someone with zero experience to quickly prepare for an entry-level position in fields such as web development, video game development, or mobile app creation within less than a year. In addition, many business degrees include specialized tracks for information technology, which can provide an entrée into a technical field with the added bonus of a business background that can boost long-term career growth prospects. Of course, a highly coveted and highly paid software engineering position at Google or Facebook will be much more likely to go to someone with at least a bachelor's degree in computer science, but today's top employers are increasingly screening for talent and putting less emphasis on the degree.

If there is any lesson we would like to repeat throughout this book, it's that career success is ultimately about what problems you can solve for others, not what kind of degree is on your résumé. If you can help solve important problems, you will be valuable, and your career success will reflect that in the long run.

Another assumption about STEM is that if you get a STEM degree, you will work in a STEM job. According to a 2011 study from the Georgetown University Center on Education and the Workforce, 58 percent of STEM graduates had moved to a career outside STEM within ten years of completing their degree.[1] In fact, about 75 percent of STEM degree holders work in a field outside STEM. What's going on? Why would someone go to all the trouble of completing a challenging science or engineering degree and then not work in a STEM career? The reason is that a STEM education can be strong preparation for success in many career fields.

Despite the immediate practicality of a STEM degree and the higher prospects for finding an entry-level job as a scientist or engineer, some people might end up outside their field of study for a number of reasons why. First, it's not uncommon that by the time a student realizes that she is not really as passionate about environmental engineering as she thought, she may be halfway or more through her degree and it would be expensive or just exhausting to change at that point. Unfortunately some college programs are better than others at giving students more practical real-world exposure to their future career early in their education. Students may not truly understand the day-to-day work of a mechanical engineer until they do a summer internship or work on real-world projects in their junior or senior year.

A second big reason for not entering a STEM career is that many industries recruit STEM graduates for nontechnical careers. A large bank, a consulting company, or even a candy manufacturer may recruit students graduating with science and engineering degrees for jobs that are nontechnical because they know that getting into a STEM degree program and finishing that degree requires a lot of raw intelligence, self-discipline, teamwork, and critical thinking skills. These are the attributes they know from experience that tend to be associated with employees in their company, and the rest of what they need they can learn on the job. Fair enough, but why would someone actually leave a STEM career? Does that indicate some kind of exodus from STEM fields that the media are not reporting?

There are at least two common reasons that someone would move out of a STEM field. Five to ten years after starting a career as an electrical engineer, biologist, or software developer, the opportunities to increase pay and get promotions may be less about your technical skills and more about your potential to combine your technical knowledge with other areas, such as management, marketing, or communications. Alternately, you may realize after a few years of exposure to the real work of your field and from talking to older people in the field that you don't see yourself enjoying the long-term career path of a dedicated scientist or technologist. And finally, in some fields, you simply can't advance much after a while without achieving some kind of major research success or winning patents for your employer. None of these reasons implies failure, and working a few years as an engineer or scientist can make you just as attractive to other types of employers.

Middle School Conversations

Now that you know some of the nuances of STEM careers, what should you discuss with your child? Middle school is often where a child truly begins to develop a meaningful and long-lasting passion for scientific or technical fields. It was the age when I began to see that there were interesting puzzles to be solved and also realized that some people were actually paid to solve them. Middle school science is just technical enough to show the beauty of experimentation, technology, and mathematical reasoning without getting overly bogged down in math. It's when kids fall in love with electric motors or astronomy or the power of making computers do their bidding with an exotic language. At this age, a small group of students will show a blazing passion for science or technology. If so, your primary job at this point is to feed that passion by exposing them to as many opportunities as possible to explore and advance their learning without discouraging them with how challenging it can be to prepare for a scientific career.

When I was in the eighth grade, I fell in love with physics. In a bout of enthusiasm, I went to my local community college and checked out a massive ten-pound textbook on nuclear physics. The next day I plunked the book down on my math teacher's desk, opened it to a page overrun with mysterious mathematical formulas, and asked, "What do all these Greek symbols mean?" The teacher replied curtly, "You don't need to worry about that right now," and it was clear that further discussion on the matter was unwelcome. This is the worst possible response, even if your child doesn't seem to be particularly good at math or science, because achieving a career in science or technology is a long-term challenge that requires enthusiasm and grit. That kind of passion will help students push through many obstacles along the way, and it's very easy in middle school for a single boring science teacher or a bad math teacher or an offhanded, dismissive remark to blow out the tiny flame of interest that could someday grow into a fulfilling career.

There are many ways that math is taught poorly in schools today, so you should never assume your child cannot do math well enough for science until you've tried to get him help. (See the additional resources section at the end of the book for some recommendations.) Unfortunately, middle school can also be a time when girls in particular begin to incorrectly perceive that deep interest or competence in science and technology might be more of a boy's thing or that all the "geeks" are boys so a girl feels unwelcome to share interests or talk shop with the others. Therefore, at this age, your primary challenge is to be on the lookout for any spark of interest in your child and keep it alight until things can get sorted more clearly in high school. If you have local programs or summer camps that teach coding, robotics, geology, or other scientific subjects, these are effective ways to nurture a budding interest with hands-on experiences that bring science to life.

Your second challenge is to make sure your child is on track with math course work or to help get her back on track if she seems to be struggling with math but remains interested in science. The ability to perform well in math and to complete advanced math such as trigonometry and calculus is usually required for pursuing a STEM degree. It is also highly correlated with successful completion of a college degree in general, so it is a good indicator of college readiness. If your child seems to enjoy science or is explicitly interested in a STEM career at this age, you can start a conversation with her that works backward in sequence from a hypothetical career to a STEM degree, to high school course work, to the choice of math course in the eighth grade.

As a general rule, students who want to pursue a STEM degree should be on track for completing calculus in high school. It may be difficult to do so without completing algebra before the end of eighth grade. Most schools and districts offer course planning software or guidebooks that will help you and your child map out a long-range plan of study for math course work through the end of high school. These tools are a great way to get your child thinking about how his near-term choices will affect his opportunities down the road. As a parent of two children, I often hear the common lament "When will I ever use this stuff I'm learning?" This is doubly true with a demanding subject like math. When responding, I try to focus on opportunities and keeping as many opportunities open as possible until they really need to make a choice. There are few other things kids can do in school that will keep more opportunities open than taking a challenging, college-prep mathematics course of study. Even if they want to study poetry at Yale, an A in calculus will give them a leg up in admissions and provide them with an analytical skill set and perspective that will likely enrich their mind and career.

What do you do if you see a strong interest in science or technology but are worried that your child is behind in math or not on track to complete algebra by the eighth grade? First, remember that math is highly dependent on foundations. Your child may be struggling with his current math course because the foundational skills that enable him to grasp that subject were taught poorly or your child struggled with that foundational concept and his teacher felt pressured to move on to the next topic (unfortunately, this is quite common due to the pressures that teachers are under to cover all the concepts taught on a state test in time for the test). You can meet with his current math teacher and ask that person directly, "Is my child weak in certain foundational skills that are necessary to be successful in his current math subject?" If the answer is yes, ask if the school can provide any resources to allow your child to review those foundational skills, seek tutoring, or seek free outside resources such as Khan Academy, a free online collection of high-quality instructional videos covering many core academic subjects.

The best kinds of discussions with your child at a younger age will be about his interests in science ("What are your favorite subjects?" "Do you want to learn more about that?") and how he is experiencing math ("Are you doing okay? Is it too easy [or too hard]? Do you think you need some help?"). If he is not already on track to complete algebra in middle school, and he has expressed genuine interest in STEM careers, you need to talk with your child and his math teacher about why and whether it's worth getting him on a faster track to support calculus in high school so that he has as many options as possible to pursue his interests in science or technology.

High School Conversations

By the end of their sophomore year of high school, students should have a solid sense of whether they can handle the mathematical and analytical rigors of science and engineering. Any deficiencies in mathematics that were due to poor teaching, rushed instruction, or learning differences should have been addressed in the freshman and sophomore years so that the final two years of high school can be focused on as much college preparatory math and science course work as the student can reasonably handle. She is running out of time to fix those and have the foundation she needs for moving forward. Don't let your child give up if she is still very passionate about science or engineering but struggling with the work. Just be prepared to get her additional support with tutoring or some of the resources listed at the end of this chapter.

This is also a good time to have more detailed discussions about your child's specific areas of interest and connect these to your child's thoughts about the importance of meaning from work and her attitudes about money. There is a spectrum of meaning and money in STEM fields. On the positive side, the average wage for all STEM occupations is approximately twice that of the average for all occupations. But there can be wide differences depending on the field and some of these differences may not make sense to a teenager yet. Seven out of the ten largest STEM occupations are related to computers, and wages in computer fields can vary dramatically. An experienced software engineer with a computer science degree from a leading university might be making well over $300,000 per year at a company like Google. But a computer systems analyst with a two-year degree in information technology may be earning less than $50,000 per year depending on her experience and location.

Your child can probably understand why there would be such a difference because the preparation and skill level for that Google engineer are at a much higher level and the competition for such a job would be intense. But what about scientists?

The average annual salary for a postdoctoral researcher in the United States is approximately $45,000. This is after competing for admission to a challenging undergraduate degree program and then completing a rigorous PhD program, during which the student barely earned enough to pay living expenses. How will that student feel watching peers graduate from less challenging academic programs and go on to earn twice as much money in half the time? This could easily be the case if one of their classmates completed a computer science degree or marketing degree from the same university. What about a life in academia as a professor or university researcher? This can seem to younger minds like an idyllic life where they can focus on the intellectual pursuits they enjoy and not be distracted by more practical concerns. Tenured teaching positions at top research universities, however, are intensely competitive and may take years of teaching at smaller colleges and constant pressure to publish new research. Scientific research grants are also highly competitive, and the funding for research scientists dependent on grant money for their job may literally be up for grabs by some other lab every three to five years.

Students who are passionate about scientific work and driven by the meaning of that work should know about some of the challenges they may face and the time horizon of achieving that dream. This is not meant to discourage them at all. Rather it is meant to help prevent them from getting discouraged because they will have given prior thought to what matters to them and will know that these are issues they may encounter if they choose the path of true scientific work. The silver lining in this potential cloud is that people who are smart enough to be in this situation will be smart enough to pivot their career if they come to realize that they want to earn money faster or take their career in a different direction. There are plenty of physics and math majors who have high-paying jobs in other fields because these are smart, analytical, hard-working people. Instead of worrying that they may not achieve their dreams of scientific discovery, young people who are interested in STEM should feel that they will wind up with a great education no matter what.

Superskills

We have just discussed how a quality STEM education will provide an excellent foundation for many careers both inside and outside STEM fields. But if you really want to help your child turbocharge her long-term career opportunities and immunize her from the perils of automation, recessions, mergers, and research funding shortages, you should talk to her about how to combine "superskills" with her STEM knowledge and interests. Software coding is a superskill. For example, we are in an unprecedented time of opportunity to apply software to problems other than selling software for its own sake or building photo-sharing applications. Many of the smartest entrepreneurs and venture capitalists believe that the big growth engine of the next fifty years will come from bringing software together with other technologies to dramatically improve productivity or solve problems we once thought were not possible to solve. Self-driving cars are a classic example of artificial intelligence software embedded within driving hardware to provide a transportation solution that once seemed like it would only ever be science fiction. This revolution is not limited to machines. It's also happening in biology, medicine, and many other fields.

Some of the most recent start-ups participating in Ycombinator, Silicon Valley's hottest start-up incubator, are applying software and data science to farming, one of the oldest technologies in human history. The innovators who will be most successful in the future will be fluent with both some kind of scientific or engineering background and software development. If you have deep subject matter expertise in a technical field and fluency with applying software solutions to the problems in that field, you will be much more valuable than if you must rely on translating your ideas to others who can implement them for you.

We can tell you from our own experience building an education technology product that having the capacity to understand market problems and then immediately turning around and writing code to solve those problems ourselves made it possible for our company to move much faster and provide better solutions to our customers during the early stages of our business when we were most vulnerable to competition. This same logic applies to scientific and technical domains, not just business products.

Another superskill is communication. If you can communicate effectively with others, you can learn from people with different perspectives and see problems that others may not be aware of. If you have deep technical expertise and the ability to code, you can now quickly solve problems that others cannot solve. If you can communicate your ideas and solutions to others, you can now sell those ideas to an investor or manager, and you can lead a team of people to help scale those ideas into the real world.

A third superskill is self-directed and continuous learning. Science and technology are constantly evolving, and the areas of expertise most in demand can change rapidly. Those who know how to proactively seek out new knowledge and add new skills after entering the workplace will be more likely to advance by working on cutting-edge projects in their field or by acquiring supplemental expertise like digital marketing, which could help them in starting a business.

There are many ways to acquire new skills outside of a traditional college classroom today, especially with online courses from sites like Udacity,

Coursera, Udemy, edX, Khan Academy, and many others offered directly by colleges through their online divisions. There are even online courses about learning itself, which can help students learn more rapidly, master material more deeply, and retain information longer. Spend some time talking with your child about how he could build coding, communication, and continuous learning skills to go along with his core passion in science or engineering.

Sample Earnings Outlook

Following is a sample of 2015 median annual earnings for various jobs in science, technology, engineering, and math according to the Bureau of Labor Statistics:

- Microbiologist: $67,550
- Data scientist: $110,620
- Software developer: $100,690
- Physicist: $110,980
- Mechanical engineer: $68,142
- Actuary: $97,070

For wage information on other careers in the field not listed here and for more detailed local wage information or job prospects, we recommend using the online *Occupational Outlook Handbook* provided free by the Bureau of Labor Statistics at https://www.bls.gov/ooh/home.htm.

Keep in mind that we are showing median pay, so some people in these roles may earn substantially less and others may earn substantially more. Generally pay is higher in locations where the cost of living is higher and in fields that are growing more rapidly or require more specialization and experience. In addition to using the *Occupational Outlook Handbook* website, we recommend that your child conduct an Internet search using terms like "future job prospects for [career name]" to get the most current outlook on industry growth potential.

5

Can You Have a Good Career with a Degree in the Liberal Arts?

It took just seven words to strike fear into my parents' hearts: "I want to be a history major." Even though my father majored in English, my mother majored in communications, and both had successful careers as educators, my parents had something different in mind for me (your author, Steve). My father strongly encouraged me to get a degree in business. My mom was never quite as blunt about it, but it was clear she shared my father's anxiety that a liberal arts degree wasn't the most logical step to a successful career and—top of mind for them, I'm sure—a big enough paycheck to keep me from moving back home after graduation.

I was a pretty good student in high school. I liked most of my classes, but my favorite by far was AP American history. I took American history as a senior, and even as many of my classmates were counting the days until graduation, my history class kept me deeply engaged all year. I enjoyed the reading and writing. I loved the discussions in class each day. Intellectually, I had found a passion.

As I was applying to college, my interest in history was never far from my mind. That said, it seemed a bit impractical. I wasn't really sure what I would do with a history degree. Should I teach high school? That was an obvious career path, and in a sense teaching was the family business. My dad taught English for many years before he moved into school administration as a high school assistant principal and then principal. My mom taught first grade for nearly her entire career. They both loved teaching. But perhaps because education was such an obvious path, my parents wanted me to think more broadly about my options.

I had many interests. I loved music. I loved technology. At one point, I wanted to be an architect, going so far as to sketch (to scale) hundreds of thousands of square feet of office space I imagined building some day. So although the thought of myself as a future teacher wasn't far-fetched, it didn't seem like my calling.

With a career as a teacher seeming unlikely and without knowing much else that someone with a history degree might do, I put aside my interest in history. My parents, who were increasingly focused on future economic opportunities for me, seemed to keep coming back to the idea that I should get a degree in business.

Many colleges and universities allow students to apply without choosing a major, but that's not always the case. Cornell University, where I went, comprises seven separate undergraduate colleges. When applying, candidates choose a college, and depending on the college they pick, they may or may not have to choose a major. With my parents' interest in my future business career and my lack of a strong pull in another direction, I applied to Cornell's School of Industrial and Labor Relations (ILR), which offered a business-friendly degree. The ILR School offered another benefit. ILR is one of three undergraduate colleges at Cornell affiliated with the State University of New York. Because I was a New York State resident at the time, my ILR tuition was roughly one-third what it would have been to study music, architecture, history, or any of the other subjects taught in Cornell's four endowed undergraduate colleges that aren't affiliated with the state university.

It didn't take long for me to realize I had made a mistake. While I fell in love with Cornell and appreciated the quality of the ILR program, it wasn't for me. Of the courses I took in my first two semesters, the ones I enjoyed most focused on American labor history. After a few meetings with an academic advisor, it was clear I needed to have a conversation with my parents. My business career was taking a detour before it even started.

Making the switch from ILR to history at Cornell wasn't easy. Because history was offered through a different undergraduate college, the College of Arts and Sciences, I needed to submit an application to transfer. Fortunately the credits I earned as an ILR student could count toward my degree in history, but there were some additional requirements I'd need to fulfill, which meant I'd need to do at least one summer session to stay on track to graduate in four years. For my parents, who were paying for my undergraduate degree, the switch from ILR to Arts and Sciences meant tuition nearly tripled. The higher cost plus the perceived risk to my future employment made my history degree a tough sell to my dad. In the end, he agreed to the higher cost, thanks in no small part to my mom.

Studying history in college was a transformative experience for me. Finding something that aligned with my interests and my strengths led me to work harder than I ever had before. I developed strong relationships with faculty members who helped me to develop personally and intellectually. I even chose to do an optional thesis as a senior, which combined my interest in history with a latent interest in education to explore the development of vocational education programs in American public schools at the turn of the twentieth century. I had no idea that ten years later, I'd be cofounding an education technology company and that my senior thesis would be relevant to more than my degree.

After earning my history degree, I got a job as an instructional designer for a company that delivered training in computer applications to corporate customers. A few years later, I went back to school, earned an MBA, and then returned to the corporate world as a technology project manager. Some years later, I cofounded Naviance.

My personal story has a happy ending, as it does for many others who pursue a liberal arts degree. But the questions about the practicality and relevance of studying the liberal arts persist. The emphasis on careers in science and technology can even make subjects like language, literature, philosophy, and history seem dated and quaint. But as my own experience has taught me, a degree in the liberal arts can be fulfilling intellectually and satisfying economically.

What Are the Liberal Arts?

Before going further, it's worth taking a moment to define *liberal arts*. Dating back to medieval times, the term referred to the trivium (grammar, rhetoric, and logic) and quadrivium (arithmetic, geometry, music, and astronomy). These subjects were generally taught to those in the upper classes in society, while the less affluent studied the *servile arts*, or hands-on skills.

In current use, the term *liberal arts* is generally applied to the humanities (e.g., literature, history, music), psychology, and mathematics, which provide general knowledge and develop intellectual capacity (e.g., reason, judgment), rather than focusing on specific job-related skills. In this context, the word *liberal* comes from the Latin word *liber*, which means free or unrestricted and has nothing to do with the use of the term in politics, where it's seen as the opposite of conservative.

As you can see from this definition, the perceived tension between liberal arts and career training is nothing new. In fact, it dates back hundreds of years. Even in the United States, we have had an ongoing debate about the form schooling should take since 1852, when Massachusetts became the first state to require that all children (then up to the age of fourteen) be enrolled. By the late nineteenth century, compulsory schooling was spreading nationwide and expanding to include older children. In 1892, the National Education Association (NEA) convened the Committee of Ten, a group chaired by Charles W. Eliot, president of Harvard University, to make recommendations for what students should learn in high school. The Committee's report essentially proposed that all students, regardless of their socioeconomic background or post–high school plans, should receive a liberal arts education.

At the time of the Committee's report in 1893, only about 6 percent of children from the ages of fourteen to sixteen attended school. As compulsory education expanded nationally and as high school enrollments consequently grew ever larger and more diverse, the NEA appointed a new group, the Commission on the Reorganization of Secondary Education, which published a report of its work in 1918. By then, more than 30 percent of fourteen- to seventeen-year-olds were in school, and the Commission's conclusions stood in stark contrast to those reached by the Committee of Ten twenty-six years earlier.

The Commission on the Reorganization of Secondary Education envisioned a different type of high school—one that would change and àdapt to the needs of contemporary society and would place an explicit focus on preparation for work. The Commission's report, "Cardinal Principles of Secondary Education," proposed seven principles:

- Health
- Command of fundamental processes
- Worthy home membership
- Vocation
- Civic education
- Worthy use of leisure
- Ethical character

In the Commission's view, curricular differentiation was critical. Like the Committee of Ten a generation earlier, it expected that students of all backgrounds would attend the same school. Unlike the Committee, however, the Commission believed that children would have vastly different experiences in school, including some pathways that would be distinctly vocational.

This debate about the form and function of high school echoes the debate about the purpose of a college education. But that debate is built on something of a false premise because there is no inherent conflict between a liberal arts education and preparation for the workforce. That said, liberal arts students need to be prepared to educate their future employers about the applicability of their degrees to various work roles.

Liberal Arts as a Practical Choice

Many of today's hottest majors are in technology and business, and with good reason. Both offer a clear path to employability. What may be less obvious, though, is that the liberal arts can also be a practical, career-friendly choice.

Over the past two decades, the concept of twenty-first-century skills has gotten a lot of attention among educators. The idea is that success in society (including the workplace) now hinges on a few higher-order abilities. Various groups have their own take on which skills make the list, but at the core, most lists of twenty-first-century skills have four key concepts:

- Collaboration and teamwork
- Creativity and imagination

- Critical thinking
- Problem solving

The National Association of Colleges and Employers (NACE) conducts an annual survey of hiring managers to get their input on the skills they value most when they recruit at colleges and graduate schools. These are the ten most common responses on NACE's 2016 survey:

- Ability to work in a team (78.0 percent)
- Problem-solving skills (77.3 percent)
- Communication skills—written (75.0 percent)
- Strong work ethic (72.0 percent)
- Communication skills—verbal (70.5 percent)
- Leadership (68.9 percent)
- Initiative (65.9 percent)
- Analytical and quantitative skills (64.4 percent)
- Flexibility and adaptability (63.6 percent)
- Detail oriented (62.1 percent)

As you'd expect, there's a close linkage between twenty-first-century skills and the results of the NACE survey. What's more interesting is the close linkage between these skills, the hiring profiles employers value most, and the attributes that liberal arts majors develop in their course work.

Some colleges and universities are accelerating their own efforts to help aspiring liberal arts majors understand their career opportunities. A degree in the liberal arts, particularly when combined with complementary course work in specific areas such as business or technology, can be a powerful calling card when starting a career.

Career Pathways for Liberal Arts Majors

Because the liberal arts include a variety of academic disciplines, they offer many different pathways to success. There are liberal arts majors in virtually every line of work: law, government, medicine, education, business, computer science, and more. A solid approach for building a career pathway as a liberal arts major is to focus on a subject that interests you while seeking out other course work or experience in a job-related field. In my case, I had a lifelong interest in technology.

During summer breaks in high school, I helped my father with the computer systems at his school. I also worked as an instructor at a local computer training center. While I didn't know it at the time, those experiences turned out to be extremely helpful as I considered my career options in college. Over time, I was able to combine my passion for history, my interest in education, my experience in technology, and my desire to start a business into a career in education technology. The creativity and critical thinking skills that I honed in college formed a solid foundation for me as I developed new skills in business through experience in the workplace and his MBA course work. Even as a business school student, I continued to seek out opportunities to combine those interests and created a unique path for myself. While many of my classmates pursued traditional MBA roles in consulting or investment banking, I spent the summer between my first and second years of business school working in an engineering laboratory. While there, I learned about some interesting new technologies that we now know as the World Wide Web. That's also where I met my Naviance cofounder and coauthor, who is another liberal arts major with a personal interest in technology.

Opportunity comes in many forms and from many directions, and no two pathways will be identical. Nor will every pathway be a straight line. And that's okay. Because I had been intentional about complementing my history degree with job-related skills, I was able to take advantage of these opportunities. If I hadn't thought about my career until after I finished my degree or if I'd tried to think of my career and my degree in isolation, I might have missed out.

Famous Liberal Arts Majors

Development Dimensions International, a global management consulting firm that focuses on leadership development in business, released a study in 2016, "High-Resolution Leadership," that found liberal arts majors are especially well equipped to be business leaders. The study looked at data from more than fifteen thousand leaders and identified eight areas of expertise that are important to business leadership:

- Financial acumen
- Business savvy
- Compelling communication
- Driving execution

- Driving for results
- Entrepreneurship
- Influence
- Inspiring excellence

The study looked at how graduates from seven disciplines (business, engineering, law, humanities, information technology, natural sciences, and social sciences) performed in each area. Humanities majors tied business majors with each being rated as strong in five of eight areas. Business majors brought expertise in "financial acumen" and "business savvy," which humanities majors lacked. But humanities majors scored especially well on "driving for results" and "inspiring excellence." A humanities major with some formal training in business would excel in all eight areas.

Though many factors play into career choice, and no college degree can guarantee career success, it's not surprising to find many high-profile business leaders who have liberal arts degrees given the strong overlap between skills required in business and those developed through a liberal arts education. Here are a few examples:

- Ken Chenault, CEO of American Express (history)
- Howard Schultz, founder of Starbucks (philosophy)
- Richard Plepler, CEO of HBO (government)
- Carly Fiorina, former CEO of Hewlett Packard (medieval history and philosophy)
- Denise Morrison, CEO of Campbell Soup Company (economics and psychology)
- Steve Ells, chairman and co-CEO of Chipotle (art history)
- Frederick W. Smith, CEO of FedEx (economics)
- Abigail Johnson, president and CEO of Fidelity Investments (art history)
- Lloyd Blankfein, CEO of Goldman Sachs (history)
- Kenneth Frazier, CEO of Merck & Co. (political science)
- Sheryl Sandberg, COO of Facebook (economics)

If working in business isn't your thing but you still want a degree in the liberal arts, there are lots of options. Other famous liberal arts graduates include talk show host and businesswoman Oprah Winfrey (speech communications and performing arts), comedian Steve Martin (philosophy), Governor Jerry Brown of California (classics), journalist Barbara Walters (English), and former president George W. Bush (history).

If my parents had this list twenty-five years ago they might not have worried as much about whether I would ever get a good job.

Short-Term and Long-Term Salaries and the Impact of Career Choice

We hope this chapter is helping you become more comfortable with the idea that liberal arts majors can be well prepared for career success. That said, it's probably fair to say that if short-term earnings are your teen's highest priority, the liberal arts may not be the best fit.

One of the reasons that technical degrees are popular and get so much attention is that their graduates tend to earn comparatively high starting salaries. According to data provided by job market analytics firm Burning Glass, the average starting salary in 2016 for jobs traditionally open to liberal arts graduates was $42,730. Jobs for graduates with some technical skills were $6,000 higher. Jobs for graduates with data analytics skills were $13,000 higher, and for graduates with computer programming skills, they were nearly $18,000 higher.[1]

If that were the end of the story and if maximizing starting salary were at the top of your teen's priorities, you might stop there. As we try to convey throughout this book, however, one's ideal career choice is based on many factors, including interests, strengths, and a personal view of what work means. If your teen's interests and strengths align with the liberal arts and she is comfortable with the starting salaries, you may be encouraged to know that over time, liberal arts majors generally catch up to and often surpass those with professional or preprofessional degrees, although those with technical degrees do earn somewhat higher salaries overall.

The Association of American Colleges and Universities (AACU) and the National Center for Higher Education Management Systems studied long-term career and salary data for approximately 3 million U.S. residents with a bachelor's degree, which they group into four categories based on undergraduate major: humanities and social sciences; professional and preprofessional; physical sciences, natural sciences, and mathematics; and engineering. While its recent humanities graduates in their study earned less than those with professional and technical degrees, by midcareer they outearned their professional degree-holding peers and were employed at similar rates. According to the report, *How Liberal Arts and Sciences Majors Fare in Employment,* "While those with humanities or social science degrees earn nearly $5,000 less than those with professional or pre-professional degrees employed directly out of college, they earn more than $2,000 more at peak ages."[2] Engineering graduates are the highest earners on average—both immediately after graduation and later in their careers.

A key source of the salary differential comes from the career paths that graduates with different majors tend to pursue and, to an extent, the additional education required based on the chosen career. According to the same study, 50 percent of those working in social services fields such as counselors, social workers, and clergy, which tend to have relatively lower salaries than other fields requiring a college degree, hold undergraduate degrees in the humanities or social sciences. It can also be helpful to look at the most popular career paths by major. Teaching at the elementary or middle school level is the most popular profession for humanities and social sciences majors, at an average salary of just under $54,000. Management was the most popular profession for those with engineering degrees, at an average salary of just over $115,000. Among humanities and social sciences majors, four of the top twenty career choices paid an average salary of at least $100,000 compared to three of twenty for professional and preprofessional majors, nine of twenty for natural/physical sciences or mathematics majors, and fifteen of twenty for engineering majors. Looking at the top twenty career choices by major shows that no major has a monopoly on highly paid jobs.

Physicians and surgeons were highest paid among majors, with annual earnings of more than $260,000. Dentists were the second highest paid, with annual earnings of just under $153,000. Both of these career paths were among the top twenty professions for those who majored in natural/physical sciences or mathematics. But an undergraduate degree doesn't qualify anyone to work as a physician, surgeon, or dentist. Each of those careers requires a graduate degree, and in each of the four categories of majors in the study, a graduate degree led to a significant increase in average earnings. Humanities and social sciences majors with an advanced degree realized a gain in annual earnings of almost $20,000 versus those who had obtained a bachelor's degree alone.

When looking across the four categories of majors, average salary appears to align more closely with career than with college major. Despite concentrations of jobs at the higher end of the salary scale among physical/natural science or math majors, they earned salaries comparable to those of humanities and social sciences majors in similar careers. Consider elementary and middle school teachers as an example. Those with undergraduate degrees in humanities or social sciences earned just under $54,000, while those with undergraduate degrees in physical/natural sciences or math earned just under $52,000.

Although they may not earn the highest salaries immediately after graduating from college, liberal arts majors are well positioned for success in a wide array of career fields. With additional training or an advanced degree in business or a technical field, liberal arts majors can differentiate themselves from others with more specialized degrees and can often find themselves at a unique advantage when building their careers. In a separate study, the AACU found support among employers for critical elements of a liberal arts education. According to the study, 93 percent of employers believe that "a candidate's demonstrated capacity to think critically, communicate clearly, and solve complex problems is *more important* than their undergraduate major," and 91 percent of employers agree somewhat or strongly that "all students should have educational experiences that teach them how to solve problems with people whose views are different from their own."[3]

Importantly, the choice of undergraduate major doesn't necessarily determine one's career path. The Georgetown University Center on Education and the Workforce found that nearly 40 percent of bachelor's degree holders work in a profession that is not directly related to their undergraduate major. While the choice of undergraduate major may not be a limiting factor in a choice of career, the decision to attend college, and, more important, the commitment to earn a bachelor's degree or higher in any field, can have a massive impact on employment and earnings. Those who earn a bachelor's degree or higher earn nearly twice as much each year as those with a high school diploma or less. Annual earnings are only part of the story. Those with a bachelor's degree or higher turned out to be far less vulnerable to job losses during the Great Recession from 2008 to 2010.

As you and your teen consider the liberal arts and other possible majors as a pathway to a career, find a field of study that aligns with your teen's interests and strengths and provides the foundation needed to be successful. Then identify a few careers that could be appealing. Given the importance of earning a degree to future success, teens need to pick a major that they know they'll want to finish. Picking a major they don't enjoy just because the career prospects look good on paper will make it hard for them to stay engaged in courses and increase the risk for dropping out.

As for me, as soon as I made the switch to history, I knew I had made the right choice. I was excited to see in the course catalogue all of the great options I'd have in the semesters ahead. In the twenty-five years that have passed since, history turned out to be the great foundation that I hoped it could be for both my MBA and my career.

Sample Earnings Outlook

Following is a sample of 2015 median annual earnings for various jobs accessible to liberal arts majors according to the Bureau of Labor Statistics:

- Elementary/middle school teacher: $54,550/$55,860
- Lawyer: $115,820
- General manager: $97,730
- Professor: $72,470
- Top executive: $102,690
- School principal: $90,410

For wage information on other careers in the field not listed here and for more detailed local wage information or job prospects, we recommend using the online *Occupational Outlook Handbook* provided free by the Bureau of Labor Statistics at https://www.bls.gov/ooh/home.htm.

Keep in mind that we are showing median pay, so some people in these roles may earn substantially less and others may earn substantially more. Generally pay is higher in locations where the cost of living is higher and in fields that are growing more rapidly or require more specialization and experience. In addition to using the *Occupational Outlook Handbook* website, we recommend that your child conduct an Internet search using terms like "future job prospects for [career name]" to get the most current outlook on industry growth potential.

6

Can You Have a Career Helping Others without Sacrificing Your Own Needs?

My father, John Fanning, barely made it out of high school. He led a rowdy, hardscrabble life as a kid growing up in a small town nestled within the mountains of southern West Virginia. As the youngest of four brothers, he always lived in fear of his own hot-tempered father, who traveled constantly as a railroad engineer and drank heavily when he was home. He and his high school administration were rarely on good terms. Some of his teachers arranged students in rows by their grade in the class, with the worst performers in the back, so he rarely sat close to the teacher. Nevertheless, no matter how far back in the classroom he sat, he knew college would be in his future. His mother, a well-educated and determined woman, had made it clear to her sons that no matter how much mayhem they caused growing up around town, they would go off to college and earn a degree.

Determined not to let his mother down, he managed to squeak out of high school with some help from a few kind teachers. He attended a nearby college, hitchhiking to and from campus each semester. There, he soon realized that he was bright enough to succeed; he just needed to learn how to study and find a larger purpose for himself. He found in himself a deeply rooted desire to fix people, and maybe somehow fix himself as well. That purpose ultimately propelled him to complete multiple advanced degrees and spend his entire career as a leader in the health and human services field.

Having an alcoholic and violent father was a traumatic experience that shaped my dad in profound ways. It is not surprising, then, how many people working in helping professions like social work, medicine, psychology, and teaching have such stories of their own. Growing up with trauma, caring for a disabled relative, or witnessing people suffer from poverty, abuse, addiction, crime, illness, or bad schools can deeply influence one's career path. Probably more than any other area, people in the helping professions tend to feel that their work is a calling, but this can be a double-edged sword. It can create a powerful and enduring motivation to work through challenging circum-stances and to help make the world a better place. It can provide meaning and fulfillment in ways that more materialistic careers cannot. But it can also lead to disappointment and burnout if their expectations are not tempered with some realism. People can be very difficult to "fix," even when they ask for help, and not everyone wants to be helped. In this chapter, we explore topics to consider if your child has a strong interest in the helping professions.

What Are the Helping Professions?

Careers in the helping professions cover a wide range, including medicine, nursing, psychological counseling, social work, teaching, school counseling, life coaching, and even ministry. We include medical careers here, even though there can be a huge difference in education, job requirements, and earnings for, say, a neurosurgeon, compared to that of a physical therapist or nurse practitioner. Some might argue that a neurosurgeon is more of a science technology, engineering, and math (STEM) career than a helping profession. It can be, depending on focus, but the drive to enter a career field like that often comes from the same inner calling to help people. If your teen is interested in being a doctor or surgeon, it is worth reading through both this chapter and the STEM career chapter (chapter 4), given the extensive amount of science and math preparation typically required.

The core element of helping professions is that they focus on improving the emotional, intellectual, physical, or spiritual wellness of fellow human beings. Probably the biggest appeal of helping professions is the opportunity to have a tangible and direct impact on the lives of people in need. A teacher can literally watch children's minds grow through their daily lessons. A school counselor can improve the trajectory of a student's entire life just by lending an ear during a crisis. A therapist can help someone finally overcome a mental illness, enough to form friendships or start dating. An oncologist can give more years of life to a mother of four children. A child advocate can rescue children from a dangerous situation and help a family turn itself around.

How many of us in other professions can say that we change lives and improve humanity in such a powerfully direct way? These professionals sound almost like superheroes when you think about what an impact they can have. But anyone working in these professions will tell you that it's not always that simple. They often face monumental challenges from surprising sources, they do not always succeed with everyone they help, and they can feel unappreciated or underpaid for their work. Despite these obstacles, plenty of people get immense personal fulfillment from their role in helping others. Like any other career field, the helping professions have their potential rewards and their potential downsides. We discuss both so that your child will have a better ability, in planning her future education and career pathway, to compare this pathway to others.

Educational Preparation

Although there are exceptions, it is difficult to enter most helping professions without at least a bachelor's degree. For example, all states require a K–12 teacher to hold a bachelor's degree. There are entry-level caretaker positions that do not require a bachelor's degree, but these tend to be hourly positions that require shift work. They start at a pay level not much different from that for retail service jobs and are not likely to provide good benefits. Fields such as social work, child psychology, school counseling, nurse midwifery, family and marriage counseling, speech pathology, special education teaching, occupational therapy, and church ministry all require at least a four-year degree and often a specialized degree or certification for an entry-level career.

Nursing is one profession, in particular, where you can enter the field with an associate degree. If your child is thinking about nursing but isn't sure how far he wants to go in that field, one option could be to complete an associate degree and get some work experience as a licensed practical/ vocational nurse or registered nurse (some states may require a bachelor's degree). Then if he enjoys the work and wants to advance, he can go back to school and complete a four-year degree, and potentially a master's degree, to become a more technically trained nurse and increase his earning potential.

Unless students are very certain they want to go straight to medical school or a master's program, it is generally a good idea to get an undergraduate four-year degree with a specialization that will support direct entry into a specific helping profession. A bachelor of social work (BSW) for example, is far more useful in finding a specific entry-level job than a bachelor of psychology, which is much more of a broad survey of the field of psychology and not specific preparation for practical work. A student can still go from earning a bachelor of psychology directly into a master of social work (MSW) degree program, but that presumes she is very confident that she wants to work in the social work field. She also should have had some practical internships and experiences before making that commitment. If your child aspires to be a teacher, typically a state requires that he major in the area in which he intends to teach. It could be wasteful to get a bachelor's degree in sociology if he knows he wants to teach middle school science, because he may then need to pay for additional course work to qualify to teach that subject.

Young people who are interested in attending medical school after they complete their undergraduate degree may believe they must major in a biological science or a premed pathway. Most colleges do not have a specific premed major, and there are plenty of students accepted by medical schools who did not study biology. There are biological science requirements within medical school, of course, and undergraduate biochemistry majors have an easier time with those requirements. However, if they chose to study physics or astronomy instead because they were also interested in those fields, they would likely be able to manage their science requirements in medical school just fine. Remember that medicine is not just about treating physical diseases or medical procedures. It can involve diverse subjects such as medical ethics and psychiatry, or even be focused on areas like mathematical modeling and statistical science. Students with many different educational backgrounds and interests end up in medical school. Regardless of what your child studies, it will be important to have a strong grade point average from her under-graduate course work when applying to medical school. She should be aware of this and prepared to make the commitment to achieving it.

Long-term Career Growth

Within the helping professions, it may be difficult for practitioners to advance their career and increase their earning potential over the long run much without a master's degree or doctorate. Unfortunately, a lot of entry-level and practitioner roles do not support a very high standard of living, at least as a single individual. It is common to get a bachelor's degree, acquire a few years of experience, and then return to school for a master's degree. There is often flexibility here, though, in changing career focus. For example, your child might work as a nurse, then start volunteering to go on pro bono medical missions in a poverty-stricken area, then decide to get a master's degree in public health and begin working for a nonprofit that helps advance legislation related to health care for the poor. For those who want to move into supervisory roles or begin an advanced and more lucrative practice such as clinical psychology, moving past a bachelor's degree is essential.

One other common way of advancing a career is transitioning into private practice as a sole practitioner, part of a group private practice, or ultimately opening your own set of facilities as a founder. This comes with another set of challenges, though, that have little to do with helping people, and a lot to do with running a business. We cover those challenges in chapter 7 on business careers and entrepreneurship, but in general, it means spending much less time helping people directly as a practitioner, which was the original drive for getting into the field. Yet it also may dramatically increase earnings.

My father worked for twenty years practicing, and supervising, within public mental health and substance abuse programs, with a specialized expertise in helping the intellectually disabled. He opened one of the first group homes for the intellectually disabled in the state of Virginia and was the vanguard of a larger movement to transition them out of prisonlike institutions and into smaller homelike environments. He was proud of his work and was paid well enough to provide our family with a solid middle-class lifestyle. By the time he reached middle age, though, he had grown weary of dealing with a board of directors and the constant political battles that come with leadership in public service. He realized that his temperament was better suited to private practice. He then established his own facility for intellectually disabled adults with severe behavioral issues and within five years had opened six group homes and increased his income substantially over his pay as a public supervisor. This was not easy, and it helped to have his experience in public service. Because he had a master's degree and twenty years of experience, and had written books, consulted, and given speeches in his field, opening a private facility was easier than it would have been if he had tried to do it only a few years out of college. That experience was crucial to avoiding many of the perils of private business within helping fields such as intense regulatory scrutiny, sudden rule changes that can immediately hit the bottom line, and potential lawsuits stemming from employee mistakes. Also, it still required business skills like marketing, sales, managing money, hiring, firing, and random things like getting sprinklers installed in an older home. It has at times been a stressful journey for him. Today, however, he can still say that through his work, he helps disabled people live a more dignified life, while also enjoying the financial fruits of his willingness to take risks and work very hard—a true win-win.

Practical Challenges

Working in a helping profession can be highly rewarding, but it is helpful to go in with an awareness of some of the factors that can cause stress and dissatisfaction with these careers. Whether those factors end up affecting your child personally very much depends on his specific circumstances, motivations, and temperament. Let's look at some of the most common sources of frustration.

First, there is a difference between studying something in college and doing it in practice. This is especially true for helping professions because of the deeply personal calling that may have drawn your child to it. In many cases, the challenging reality is that these are jobs in which practitioners deal with human suffering while getting paid on the lower end of the spectrum. This may sound obvious, but we humans are very good at fooling ourselves by thinking only of the positive aspects of something and discounting the negative. This is true especially when we have built dreams of our possible future. Like any of the other career fields we discuss in this book, it really helps for students to find opportunities to try on a career before investing too much.

It's very important to try, as much as possible, to get an inside look at the daily realities of a helping profession before committing to the required education or to an employer. In some of these professions, it can be very tough to find qualified people, like teachers in a poor urban community. Employers will be investing heavily to find, train, and support new employees, so anyone pursuing this path should know something about what to expect. Many helping professions require that practitioners already have some practical experience before applying, so a lot of degree programs build that into their curriculum, but these opportunities may not come until later in any degree program. Maybe your child will not be offered student teaching positions until junior or senior year. Using the techniques we discuss in chapter 10, students can still get more insight into the real-world experience of being a teacher before they are required to fully commit to that degree path.

Another challenge can be the degree to which job prospects, job requirements, and pay are subject to turbulent changes in politics, public policy, or state budgets. Teachers, for example, have had to adjust to major new curriculum policy changes such as the Common Core State Standards, yet in many cases, they have not been given adequate professional development on effective ways to deliver instruction that adheres to the new standards. This change is only one of many new requirements that come and go depending on changes in federal education policies, state education policies, and district leadership. In addition, the teaching profession itself has come under broad criticism from major policy institutes, funding organizations, business leaders, and journalists.

While there is no doubt that some teachers are not effective and teacher training and certification could improve their skills, it has still been demoralizing for truly excellent teachers with years of success to feel painted with the same brush of mediocrity. Some have been blamed for student failures that often have as much to do with deeply rooted structural issues like poverty, school funding, and racism as anything else. When a person's profession comes under that kind of public scrutiny, it can drain their motivation and distract from their core mission of helping students.

Some of these helping professions, such as teaching, are commonly public-sector jobs, which means wages and benefits may be public information and subject to political conditions. It can feel disorienting and invasive to have one's compensation be such a public matter of debate. Being in private practice doesn't guarantee freedom from these challenges either. Public policy changes can just as easily hit entrepreneurs in the helping professions.

My father's business is highly dependent on Medicaid funding to cover the cost of housing, feeding, medicating, and supervising the intellectually disabled adults in his group homes. Yet he is frequently subject to unexpected changes in how much Medicaid funding will be provided per person, what types of services must be provided in exchange for that, what type of documentation is required, how many staff members must be present in certain situations, and how many individuals may reside in a facility.

Imagine if you ran a restaurant and city officials could come in at any time and tell you that they are changing half of the rules that govern how you run your business, affecting who you hire and how much money you make. In addition, you will be fined or shut down if you do not comply quickly. Many of these rules are there for good reasons (like ensuring safety or preventing abuse), and many of these changes are made because of unsustainable cost increases or better guidelines for care. But when your business is required to spend $100,000 to comply with new regulations, will you have it in the bank? The state legislature and regulatory agencies will not be able to bend the rules just for you.

Emotional Risks

One of the most profound challenges of helping others is the emotional weight of it. Nurses and doctors may deal with sickness and death every day. Social workers will see the myriad ways in which people suffer from mental illness. Child services case workers see the most vulnerable members of our society treated in horrifying ways. Teachers endure stressed-out parents struggling to manage their children with attention deficit hyperactivity disorder or learning differences. Alcohol rehabilitation counselors work with good people who have unwittingly destroyed an entire family.

In addition to the suffering that your child, as a practitioner in these fields, may observe in others they are trying to help, they may have to grapple with the fact that they do not always successfully end that suffering when given the opportunity. Not every therapy patient learns to manage a mental illness, not every student graduates, and not every alcoholic maintains sobriety after treatment. Sometimes the reasons for this are the people around that person whom helping professionals cannot control, such as an abusive parent, a dysfunctional spouse, an administrator playing politics, or a criminal justice system with endemic racism. That may seem like an obvious part of the job to your child, but if he is seriously considering a helping profession, it's likely because he is naturally empathetic to others. Yet this empathy can turn on him if he does not learn to manage his own reactions to the suffering around him.

It's important for people in the helping professions to care for themselves as well. Often they will be in roles where it feels that their own needs must come last. A minister providing pastoral counseling to a dying member of her congregation at 2:00 a.m. may wonder, "What else could be more important than this?" A teacher in a striving inner-city middle school may get text messages at 9:00 p.m. from a student desperate for help with a reading assignment and wonder how she is going to bring these kids up from a third-grade to an eighth-grade reading level. A conscientious emergency room doctor may feel compelled to stay even after a long shift to check on a patient who really worries her. The inability to set personal boundaries and take care of one's own needs will lead to burnout, a phenomenon that is common in the helping professions. A social worker, teacher or nurse will have family members and friends who need time from them too, and those special bonds are what ultimately sustain all of us.

We should make a special note here regarding medicine. Not only can the daily practice of medicine require a lot of time and energy from someone (depending on the field), but training can take many years. During those years, it may be challenging for your child to get married and have children if that is his goal. Recent regulatory changes now allow medical residents to work twenty-four-hour shifts. Obviously anyone working a lot of those long and tiring shifts is not spending much time with a significant other or a child or even pursuing a hobby.

For almost all the helping careers that potentially expose practitioners to burnout, there are well-established ways to move into less emotionally or physically taxing parts of the field. We do not mean to imply that everyone is headed for a burnout experience. An option is to move into supervision or management, although this typically requires going beyond a bachelor's degree to get a master's degree or PhD, and this work doesn't suit everyone's temperament. But there are other pathways besides management. For example, a nurse could move from a stressful job in a hospital with irregular shift work to a 9-to-5 nursing position with a private rehabilitation facility. In this position, she might be on call less frequently and have vacation and sick leave similar to someone working at a more traditional job.

A related trap that sometimes befalls professional helpers is bringing their own suffering to work. As we noted, many people come into a helping career because they experienced trauma or witnessed suffering. It's important that those individuals ensure they get the kind of therapy or counseling they need to address their own experiences, or they can find themselves approaching their work in unhealthy ways. Even years into professional practice, proper supervision and case consultation are critical in order to maintain balance and manage the potential emotions that can be transferred between a practitioner and a patient. If your child feels a deep calling to this world because of some trauma, discuss with her whether her need to help others might also be addressed by getting help for herself to ensure she is not trying to use her career as personal therapy. Anyone going into a helping profession should have clear boundaries between the satisfaction of doing the work and the need for her own treatment or personal care.

It is also essential to adhere closely to the boundaries and code of ethics established for your chosen profession. Many fields have some standard code of ethics, but this can be uniquely challenging for people in helping careers because they are involved in such deeply human and personal situations. Often it is the person who is trying the hardest to help someone else who steps over a boundary, not the stereotype of some predator we might imagine trying to take advantage of them (though this does happen). If your child does informational interviewing or job shadowing as we recommend in chapter 11, he should inquire about the kinds of boundaries and ethical codes that are important in his field of interest to gain a better sense of whether he can manage them.

Finally, most of these professions require continuing education. Teachers, therapists, counselors, doctors, and many others need to return to the classroom every so often to stay up-to-date with the latest research and best practices in their field. That doesn't always mean sitting in a classroom with a professor. Often it can be workshops and conferences that are provided by industry groups and consultants. This demonstrates a commitment to lifelong learning as part of the profession. For some, this can be an appealing part of the job. Some fields of medicine are evolving rapidly, and exciting research is coming out all the time that could potentially save more lives. It can be fun to be on the cutting edge and keep from getting bored by always learning something new. For others, though, this could be a source of frustration, especially if your child has learning differences and struggles with school. That doesn't mean it is not worth overcoming to achieve goals, but it's something to think about if he is exploring a helping profession and trying to better understand his potential career experiences.

We hope this chapter has given you and your child a lot to discuss. Both of us have been deeply touched by people in the helping professions who have cared for our parents, our friends, and our children. There are doctors who gave people we love extra life and precious extra time with them. There are teachers who believed in us and challenged us to be better than we realized we could be. We owe a great debt to them, and you should be proud of your child for wanting to walk in their footsteps. Maybe this book will help you give her that extra nudge, or food for thought to overcome her doubts, and make the world a better place.

Sample Earnings Outlook

Following is a sample of 2015 median annual earnings for various jobs in the helping professions according to the Bureau of Labor Statistics:

- Home health aide: $21,920
- Physical therapist: $84,020
- Registered nurse: $64,790
- Emergency medical technician/paramedic: $31,980
- Physician/surgeon: $187,200
- Dentist: $158,310
- Nutritionist: $57,910
- High school teacher: $57,200
- Preschool teacher: $28,570
- Social worker: $45,900
- Rehabilitation counselor: $34,390

For wage information on other careers in the field not listed here and for more detailed local wage information or job prospects, we recommend using the online *Occupational Outlook Handbook* provided free by the Bureau of Labor Statistics at https://www.bls.gov/ooh/home.htm

Keep in mind that we are showing median pay, so some people in these roles may earn substantially less and others may earn substantially more. Generally pay is higher in locations where the cost of living is higher and in fields that are growing more rapidly or require more specialization and experience. In addition to using the *Occupational Outlook Handbook* website, we recommend that your child conduct an Internet search using terms like "future job prospects for [career name]" to get the most current outlook on industry growth potential.

7

Do You Want to *Work* in Business or *Be* in Business?

I (Shaun) have never been a fan of the word *business* and especially the term *business major*. It sounds so ordinary and boring. Yet there are businesses today that are curing diseases, delivering supplies to the International Space Station, and helping wounded veterans walk again. Even if your work is in marketing, finance, public relations, or sales, it's no less exciting to be involved in something like that and do your special part to help it succeed. On the flip side, the terms *entrepreneur* and *start-up* sound sexy. They convey a vision of hustle, big dreams, and money. But I've been an entrepreneur and met hundreds more of them over the years, and the reality can be more like grueling work that cuts deeply into your personal life, dark days when you're not sure how you will pay your employees, and no guarantee of success even if you're lucky enough to raise money from investors. Today more than any other time in our history, the idea of entrepreneurship has become a prestigious pursuit, so much so that magazines love to write sensationalized articles about entrepreneurs who dropped out of Harvard or Stanford to pursue their dreams.

In this chapter we explore business, entrepreneurship, and the kinds of experiences and educational programs that can prepare someone for these pathways. We also discuss some of the misconceptions about entrepreneurship and how to help your child explore entrepreneurship as a potential pathway.

Between the two of us, we have spent a combined total of about fifty years in business. We have worked for Fortune 500 companies and multinational conglomerates and have started businesses from scratch with our credit cards. We have hands-on experience with corporate strategy, product management, marketing, sales, customer service, consulting, contract negotiation, patent law, public relations, financial modeling, accounting, software development, quality assurance, management, leadership, human resources, public speaking, outsourcing, mergers and acquisitions, partnership development, and still more. We have personally participated in all of these and have also hired people to do them, fired people who didn't do them well, and made judgment calls about how to do them better.

We have at times been wildly successful and at other times fallen flat on our faces. None of our success would have happened without the help of many others working for us, alongside us, and above us. If there is a pattern we can identify about what made the greatest impact, it has little to do with what we studied in college. Of course, good marketers are good in part because they've learned their craft, and good data scientists must obviously have studied hard to learn the intricacies of data science. But their success had more to do with how they applied this knowledge in the real world of business, which is messy and full of people with competing strengths, motives, and needs. Book knowledge is necessary in certain roles, but it only gets one so far. Long-term successful careers in business are built more on how one handles early experiences in the workplace and whether one takes advantage of those early opportunities to learn, push beyond the comfort zone, and connect with mentors who can share hard-earned wisdom. So how can your child get started?

Educational Preparation

One of the great things about business as a career pathway is that there are many different ways to get started. Your child might assume that if she wants to be in business, she must get an undergraduate degree in business, accounting, or marketing. However, as we discuss in other chapters, anyone can just as easily enter the world of business with a degree in physics or history. As your child contemplates a business career, encourage her to think about her true interests and whether those align with specific business skills or more general areas. Accounting can be surprisingly complex and intellectually challenging for someone who is analytical and enjoys working with numbers. But it's a mistake to assume that because every business needs accounting services this is a practical degree. If your child feels no underlying interest in the topic or shows no signs of enjoying math or numerical analysis, she will likely find herself wishing she had studied something else. If she is hard-working and intelligent, she could study something more interesting to her without limiting her long-term career prospects in business.

There are opportunities for teenagers to experience some aspects of business, and we would strongly encourage any who are interested in business to get some experience to validate that interest. My twelve-year-old daughter, for example, decided to create a charity fundraising baking club in her middle school. She has never expressed an explicit interest in being in business, but the baking club has provided a remarkable range of experiences that have given her a taste of a career in business. She has had to recruit other members, estimate demand depending on location and weather, verify food vending regulations, assign responsibilities, sell products, keep track of costs and earnings, estimate cash needed from the bank, and deal with other club members who frequently fail to deliver what they promise and argue over her leadership decisions.

Early Experiences

There are all kinds of clubs, activities, and experiences that can give kids an early sense of where their interests and talents in business may lie. As you help your child explore potential opportunities to experience activities or develop skills relevant to her interest in business, here are specific things you might seek:

- *Selling and marketing.* Some people will tell you that great products sell themselves. They might point to Steve Jobs and Apple as an example of a company that makes incredible products with exquisite attention to detail and how Apple is one of the most valuable companies in the world. But don't be fooled. Steve Jobs was a master salesman and a genius at marketing. There is an expression in business circles that sales fix everything. Anyone who can tell great stories and effectively pitch a product or service will be highly valuable in business. Can your child find activities where he needs to sell things in person or on the phone? Can he be responsible for marketing an event or fundraising? Can he work on a grant proposal for a school garden or pitch an idea from the class council to school administrators?

- *Project management.* Being highly organized as an individual is a big achievement. Getting a group of people organized to accomplish something together successfully is a miracle. We have encountered a few people in our careers who can pull off that miracle on a daily basis, and this skill is highly prized. Few things happen in the world of business without a team effort, and larger organizations in particular require a lot of coordination and discipline to keep things running. Can your child find activities where she needs to figure out who is best at doing specific tasks and help keep projects on track? Can she manage a club, organize an event, or coordinate a large project?

- *Communication.* The lifeblood of a successful business is effective communication. Even if you work in a highly technical area, you will be more valuable and more likely to advance if you can communicate ideas fluently, persuade decision makers, and distill complex information into a more digestible format. Expert accountants will be more helpful if they can explain to nonaccountants why something matters to the business. Talented operations engineers will be more likely to advance into management if they are good at presenting information to company leaders or sharing expertise at industry conferences. Can your child find activities that require him to hone his communication skills, like being on a debate team or becoming a student/faculty liaison? Can he find an opportunity to present his ideas in front of other students in a class or take responsibility for preparing a slide presentation for a group project?

- *Managing money.* Financial literacy is obviously useful for anyone working within a business or owning a business. Truthfully it's useful for everyone, but learning more about it can be a great way for kids to appreciate one of the most exciting aspects of business, making money, and one of the most challenging aspects, spending less than you make. You would be surprised how many entrepreneurs today don't seem to grasp this most basic rule of business. Through managing money, your child can learn that counting money properly and allocating its use carefully is important and sometimes challenging. Can your child find activities that require her to keep track of money flows, like a club with a budget or a fundraising project? Can she start a small side business selling her services or a product that other kids might want to buy? It can be tempting for adults to take over money management when kids are involved, but try to be the one who verifies things are correct rather than the one doing all the work of keeping track.

- *Creativity.* It may come as a pleasant surprise to your child that he can take a talent or hobby and turn it into a business. Design, art, music, writing, crafts, cooking, fashion, even an obsession with sneakers can turn into a successful business that allows someone to pursue a passion and a living at the same time. Your child may have no interest in starting a business, but the ability to create can be a magic ingredient in a business career. Some of the most successful businesses come from combinations of people who are creative and people who have operational business skills. And for those with an entrepreneurial bent, it's much easier to learn those operational business skills than to learn how to be creative. Can your child experiment with selling her creative output or services? Other kids are often an enthusiastic and forgiving first market to test skills and experience the thrill of having others pay for one's creative work. Could you help your child set up an online store or a presence in an online craft marketplace like Etsy?

A Word about Automation

There was a time when automation with computer software and robotics was mainly a threat to blue-collar occupations such as manufacturing. That time has long since passed. JPMorgan recently announced the rollout of new artificial intelligence software to interpret and review commercial loan agreements. This software can now do what loan officers and lawyers spent over 360,000 hours a year doing for JPMorgan previously.

Many of the occupations that fall squarely within the business field of study are facing significant changes through automation from software or the combination of software and cheap labor overseas. Some economists argue that this increase in productivity will allow companies to invest more, grow faster, and hire more employees or possibly create new kinds of jobs. Others have raised the alarm bells with claims that vast numbers of white-collar jobs will be automated out of existence within twenty to fifty years. Having worked as corporate executives ourselves, living the daily pressure to increase our revenues, control costs, and be innovative, if we were in a position to accomplish any of those with automation, it was our responsibility to seriously consider doing so. If your competition can move faster, provide better service, and charge less, then you will not be in business much longer. According to JPMorgan, its move to automate contract renewal was driven primarily by a need to stay ahead of aggressive competitors and innovate, not reduce costs.

So how do kids know what skills or careers may fall victim to automation, and how can they future-proof themselves? One of the biggest indicators of whether an occupation is vulnerable to automation is the presence of rules or patterns. Computers are very good at following rules—for example, accounting rules, construction regulations, or commercial contract law. If a job primarily involves being trained to understand a set of rules and then repeatedly use those rules to review, edit, or flag some issue, computers can likely take over that task. This is happening a lot with rote financial and legal tasks, but any field that incorporates rules is vulnerable to the extent that a job in that field involves a lot of rule checking and not a lot of experiential judgment—although even judgment can theoretically be automated if it involves reliable patterns. Computers are very good at finding patterns, even when human beings are not yet aware that such patterns exist. For example, computer software can now "train" itself by reading or viewing millions of images; once it learns patterns, it can apply those patterns to make highly reliable guesses. The software could look at thousands of images of breast cancer biopsies and the history of whether each was malignant or not. Once it has trained on these case histories, it may be better than a human being at reading biopsies and providing a diagnosis to a patient. It may even be better than a human doctor at guessing the type of treatment most likely to cure the cancer.

How do those who are starting out in business education and career inoculate themselves from the threat of automation? Here are several strategies:

- *Learn to communicate.* Sharing ideas, persuading others, distilling complex information, presenting to groups and teaching, and providing constructive feedback are all highly valuable in a business career and will set apart the "bean counters" from the people who end up being invaluable members of a team and company.
- *Excel at teamwork.* Communication is part of teamwork, but there are other skills of effective team members. These are soft skills like empathy,

an ability to listen, an ability to make others feel heard and understood, and an openness to other points of view.

- *Develop creative skills.* Computers are very bad at invention. This is a decidedly human strength. Jobs that require creative thought and problem solving will be difficult to automate. Marketing is an obvious one, but even financial services careers can involve a good deal of creativity to develop ways of funding projects, new financial instruments for managing risk, or creative deal structures to fix a merger that has stalled.
- *Learn to lead.* Computers cannot develop an inspiring vision, spread that vision throughout a department or company, and build or mentor a team of uniquely talented individuals to achieve that vision.
- *Acquire specialized knowledge that other businesspeople may not have.* This could be a law degree, high-technology skills, or knowledge of other cultures and languages.

You can also encourage your child to read online about the fields that interest her and to search for articles about automation and artificial intelligence in business journals and magazines. This will give her a better sense for how certain career fields are evolving and what the cutting edge of that field looks like. It may also help her learn about other career fields she might want to explore in college. This is one of the reasons I chose to attend the university that I did. There were many other excellent STEM programs I could have studied if I decided not to pursue my original intended field. Students should apply the same thought process to a business education and look for educational opportunities that will allow them to build a more diversified skill set or explore a wider range of career options.

Entrepreneurship

We have already mentioned entrepreneurship a few times. There is a never-ending debate about whether entrepreneurship skills are something you are born with or something you can learn. We have seen so many different types of entrepreneurs that we don't think there is a single type of person who is successful at it. There are inborn traits that can help, like self-confidence, charisma, or self-discipline, but these same traits can just as easily be your undoing if you are not careful. What we have learned is that the best ingredient for success is experience. There is no better teacher and no better way to know if you really have what it takes or enjoy doing it.

At some point, your child may express a very tangible entrepreneurial goal. Maybe he wants to open a restaurant or bakery. Maybe she wants to build custom homes or open a massage therapy studio. Or maybe he wants to build the next Facebook or Uber. Is there anything you can talk about now, as your child is poised to move into early adulthood, that can help him increase the odds of success in the long run? We believe so.

As we discuss later in this book, it can be incredibly valuable and save a lot of angst and money in the long run if kids can find ways to "try on" a career before investing in a lot of preparation or taking a job in that field. This is particularly true with entrepreneurship, which can involve highly stressful financial risks and long work hours. Some degree programs do a great job of providing the kind of exposure that could be helpful to a future entrepreneur. Hospitality, hotel, and restaurant management programs, for example, often include direct experience in restaurants and hotels and provide networks of alumni to help students obtain practical internships that will be valuable in sampling certain aspects of business ownership.

A key concern with business ownership is that owners inevitably need to wear many hats. Often a passion in creating something (e.g., software products, ad designs, wedding cakes) will draw someone into business ownership, but it will be the challenges of sales, marketing, and cash management that can spit neophytes back out with bitter disappointment. For those going the entrepreneurial route, it's important to get some exposure to how these parts of a business or industry work.

Let's say your child gets a job as a prep chef in a local restaurant and has expressed a desire to be a chef someday with her own restaurant. Encourage her to ask the restaurant owner or manager questions about how they run the business. How do they market and find new customers? How long did it take for the restaurant to become profitable? How often are they having to hire new cooks and wait staff? What are their biggest challenges as a restaurant owner? Did they have to raise money from an investor to start out? Not every business owner will welcome these questions, but many will be happy to share and may even take the rare opportunity to vent their frustrations, which will be enlightening, to say the least. And even asking these questions of a manager at a big retail chain like The Gap, Home Depot, or McDonald's will teach kids something useful for understanding how a business runs.

What if your teen feels strongly that he wants to do a Silicon Valley–style technology start-up, either in college or immediately after? Maybe he is a technical whiz with some actual experience or already has an idea. As long as there are business magazines to be sold, there will be tales told of students who started a technology company in high school or college and went on to take over the world. It does happen, and if your child is lucky enough to have figured out how to do something that a lot of people want and will pay good money for, then by all means, he should go for it. Great business ideas don't come along every day.

More than likely, though, the real situation is that your child has some technology skills or related interests and wants to "do a start-up," "have a start-up," or "create a company." This is not how successful companies are usually born. Great companies are usually born when someone figures out that there is a problem in the world that nobody else is solving well or that could be solved in a much better way and just happens to be in a good position to fix that. Typically that means knowing a lot about this problem, the kinds of people who have this problem, or the technologies that would solve this problem. Successful entrepreneurs want to make things that people want. They like solving problems for people, not just being an entrepreneur. For this reason, we recommend that you encourage your child to work for someone else for at least a few years before starting a business. Here are the potential benefits of this route:

- *Development of stronger skills or expertise.* There is only so much your child can learn about software development or any other skill through school or side projects. Working full-time for a company that must deliver products and services at a professional level can teach knowledge about a craft that is typically only transferred from person to person. Also, a company often pays for its employees to attend industry conferences or professional development courses so they can develop those skills on the company's dime instead of their own.
- *Familiarity with potential customers.* Working for a larger company in the industry may provide an opportunity to meet many different types of customers in that industry and develop relationships. These relationships could provide initial leads for a new business or critical references and introductions. Entrepreneurs often mistakenly believe their biggest challenge will be creating a great product or service, only to realize later that they needed to spend far more time on marketing and finding

customers. Building up knowledge of where future customers network with their peers and learn about new services will give budding entrepreneurs an advantage.

- *Exposure to different domains and problems.* Some of the best business ideas come from unique insights that would make sense only to someone with a lot of experience in a narrow industry or occupation. It's a good idea because no one else has that perspective on how to solve it. Working for other companies can provide valuable knowledge about different industries or new technologies. Employees may even discover an opportunity within a unique segment of their company's clients.

- *Savings from working when living expenses are lower.* It may be possible for recent college graduates with strong technical or business skills and a well-paying job to save a significant amount of money for a few years and build a financial cushion that could enable them to take a risk on starting a business or provide critical start-up investment.

- *Increased credibility with investors.* Investors will tell others repeatedly that they invest in teams, not ideas, and that the execution of an idea is far more important than the idea itself. If a young entrepreneur already has a mobile app with millions of users, then their age and inexperience will not be an obstacle to raising money. For the vast majority, though, investors will be hesitant to invest in someone who has no meaningful experience in their field and lacks credibility. Working for a larger company can provide the experience to present ideas with more confidence and polish and perhaps even meet early-stage investors.

- *Network of potential partners, employees, or mentors.* It may come as a surprise to a new entrepreneur that recruiting other people to join their company is not as easy as posting a job ad online. Most potential employees prefer job stability and higher pay in the near term rather than uncertainty and a promise of a big payday later. It helps if those who are going to compete with established companies for employees have built a network of people within the industry who may serve as a source of leads for hiring or mentorship.

- *A fallback plan.* Knowing that you have experience and success working for others will give you the confidence that if your new venture fails, you can recover and find employment again. If you have worked hard to deliver value and get along with others, your former employer or related employers will very likely be glad to welcome you back. Great talent is always in short supply.

In this chapter, we have shown how diverse business careers can be and how many educational and job pathways can lead to success in business as an employee or an entrepreneur. Our own careers have taught us that while education can open doors to many business careers, what your child learns on the job, how well your child works with others, and how hard your child works will be far more important in the long run.

Sample Earnings Outlook

Following is a sample of 2015 median annual earnings for various jobs in the business field according to the Bureau of Labor Statistics:

- Accountant: $67,190
- Financial analyst: $80,310
- Loan officer: $63,430
- Marketing manager: $124,850
- Public relations specialist: $56,770
- Retail sales: $22,040
- Manufacturing sales: $59,080
- Information systems manager: $131,600
- Food service manager: $48,960
- Sales manager: $113,860
- Senior executive: $102,690

For wage information on other careers in the field not listed here and for more detailed local wage information or job prospects, we recommend using the online *Occupational Outlook Handbook* provided free by the Bureau of Labor Statistics at https://www.bls.gov/ooh/home.htm.

Keep in mind that we are showing median pay, so some people in these roles may earn substantially less and others may earn substantially more. Generally pay is higher in locations where the cost of living is higher and in fields that are growing more rapidly or require more specialization and experience. In addition to using the *Occupational Outlook Handbook* website, we recommend that your child conduct an Internet search using terms like "future job prospects for [career name]" to get the most current outlook on industry growth potential.

8

Can You Make a Living as an Artist or Musician?

One of our favorite things in life is discovering that a friend or colleague has a hidden artistic passion or talent. It is like peeking into a hidden world when you watch your marketing manager on television singing at a national barbershop quartet competition or you discover that one of your mild-mannered software developers has self-published several science-fiction adventure novels. Not all of us have such artistic talent and passion, but there are far more people who possess it than earn their living from it. Art, for all its profound beauty, is not the easiest route to a fat bank account or a good health care plan. Not many artists are as fortunate as Travis Barker, the successful drummer from Blink-182, who deliberately tattooed his neck so that his prospects for getting a "real job" would be so low that he would be forced to embrace music as his only living. We hope that this chapter will give you and your teen some ways of thinking about artistic careers that do not require such drastic measures.

If you are reading this chapter, we are assuming your teen has serious aspirations to pursue art as a career. We are using the word *art* to encompass many different artistic fields, including design, drawing, painting, writing, photography, music, acting, and theater. We are also assuming you are in one of two situations, or maybe both. The first is that you want to help your child understand the realistic challenges in attempting to earn a living through art. The second is that you want to help your child find a way to pursue her dreams and succeed as an artist. We try to help you in both situations.

But before we get started, we provide a special caveat. Art, more than any other occupation, is a deeply ambiguous thing in both practice and our own minds. Physics is physics, and if you want to change it, there are only very specific ways to do so. Art, in contrast, is vast and ever changing and subjective and deeply personal. The Beatles never discussed a plan with their parents to change rock music forever. It just happened, like a lot of the greatest art does. We discuss here the challenges and practical realities of being a professional artist, but we are not trying to discourage anyone from following their dreams. If anything, we want to help true artists better prepare themselves to find a way through those challenges so they can follow that path if it is right for them.

Art for the Soul and Art for the Sale

It's fair to say that almost every form of art has commercial potential. Even poetry can be sold in a greeting card, but does your child want to write greeting cards? Maybe he wouldn't mind writing greeting cards as long as he also gets to publish his poetry, teach poetry, or share his poetry with others at a poetry slam. But then again, maybe he wouldn't mind being a freelance journalist, a copywriter, or a biologist, for that matter, if he could still pursue his artistic interests on the side in a way that was fulfilling enough.

The first task for aspiring young artists is to figure out whether their art can be a career for them or if it should remain a side passion. (We don't like using the word *hobby* because there are many people not earning a living from art who nevertheless invest a tremendous amount of energy in their art and find it to be a deeply profound part of their lives.) How does one know art can be a viable career path? There are two parts to this question. The first part is whether the daily work and lifestyle of that artistic career is something they would want to do full time, even if they are not a huge success. Earning a real living from an artistic career may involve a lot of things that do not come into play when it is a side passion. The second part is whether your child can earn enough money to meet her financial goals in life.

For the Soul

In a lot of artistic fields, most of the financial spoils go to a few highly successful artists and the businesspeople who support them. There are plenty of stories in the media about hugely successful writers, actors, DJs, singers, models, fashion designers, photographers, and others. That's because it's not interesting to write about artists who have been only modestly successful, earning a decent wage, saving for retirement someday, and living in a regular house with a regular car, just like their neighbor, an accountant.

For every musician with a top 100 hit, there are thousands of talented musicians who will never get that lucky. For every writer with a debut novel that becomes a best seller and a Hollywood blockbuster, there is an endless stream of writers who will never be a guest on late-night television shows or be interviewed on the radio. But there are writers, actors, DJs, singers, models, fashion designers, and photographers who get up every day, do very good work, and take enough money home to live as an artist and not work at something less fulfilling to them. They are a modest success.

Let's say you could give an all-knowing crystal ball to your teen. Ask your teen if that crystal ball told him right now that he would never hit the big time, never be famous or win the big awards or become rich from his art, but that he would earn an average wage for his whole life and have only modest success, would he still do it? The answer to this question should be revealing. If the answer is no, then what is more important: doing the art or becoming "successful" through it?

Of course, there are big stars who will tell you they were driven by a desire to be famous, but that doesn't mean a drive to be famous is a healthy thing. It just means they made it through a gauntlet that countless others with the same drive did not. Does your child enjoy practicing her art form every day as an ordinary part of her life? Does it feel to her like something she always wants or needs to be doing? If not, then will she be able to sustain her career if she does not achieve big-time success?

To achieve even modest success within an artistic field requires very hard work. Can your teen live with doing that work and have the only reward be that he got to live a life pursuing his artistic passion? Obviously not every musician or writer will be even a modest success. Some people are not talented enough, and some people are not willing to put in the work to learn and hone their craft. Luck plays a role as well. But we think it is healthy to have an orientation first and foremost that the pursuit of art full-time will be a career—dare we say it, a job—and if your teen feels completely deflated by that idea, then he needs to give some hard thought to why.

For the Sale

If your child thinks she can approach her artistic pursuit with a career orientation and will not be dissuaded even if she never reaches the pinnacle of her field, then she should spend some time thinking about the practical questions of how much money she can realistically make and how she would structure her work.

Working for Others

Let's first explore practicing art in a more traditional 9-to-5 position. There are plenty of full-time opportunities to practice art as a salaried employee of a larger organization. Many students have great careers working full-time for a company as a designer, animator, writer, or photographer, for example. There can be a lot of benefits to this approach. Their income will be much more stable, they likely have access to decent health care, and they can save money for retirement through a company-sponsored 401k plan. If they are sick or just need some time off, they can take that time away from work without losing pay because they did not produce anything during that time. Instead of being alone all day in a studio, they likely will have colleagues who provide them with feedback or even help them develop and grow as an artist. The company may pay them to attend professional development conferences and workshops, so they get to hone their skills at the company's expense instead of having to reach into their own pockets. They may be able to establish a network of potential mentors and customers, which could be vital if they later decide to strike out on their own as a freelancer. They may also have the opportunity to work on projects that millions of people will see. Designing a new product for Facebook or working on digital art for a Marvel movie will expose their work to the entire world. And the pay can be very good. According to Glassdoor.com, the average annual salary for an animator at DreamWorks Animation is over $116,000.

There are some challenges to this approach as well. The main downsides depend very much on your child's personality and artistic passion. Not a lot of companies will pay someone full-time to produce hip-hop music. That's a field where most people have to hustle to sell their work independently. There are also industries that used to employ full-time artists, but they have undergone tremendous economic changes and can no longer afford to employ artists at the previous level. Examples of this are writing and photography. Many magazines, newspapers, and similar organizations have had to greatly reduce full-time staff in these areas because of declining growth in their revenues and competition from online media. The Internet did create new opportunities in some of these professions but often at much lower pay or freelance only. As a result, the competition for certain well-paying full-time artistic jobs at established companies has increased greatly. Also, an artist's work in these full-time roles can be subject to a lot of meddling by managers, colleagues, and corporate agendas that may conflict with the artist's creative impulses. Sometimes in exchange for security, you must trade autonomy. That may apply even to the artist's schedule. If your child does her most inspiring work at night or works only when she feels the creative juices flowing, this could be a problem in a business that needs to integrate art into a bigger corporate process that has a lot of other dependencies and time constraints.

Working Independently

The alternative to working as a more traditional employee is to work for yourself. This can seem like a rewarding way to work and your child may imagine being able to live freely wherever in the world he wants and not be subject to a 9-to-5 routine. That is the dream, but the reality can be very different. Those who work for themselves are not just doing their art. They are also running a business, and the lifeblood of any business is sales and marketing. Even if their art is high quality, people need to be exposed to it, and that doesn't magically happen just because the art is good. They will need to spend a significant amount of time hustling for clients, marketing their work to potential buyers, or promoting themselves within online communities like YouTube. If they are marketing themselves, there will also probably be a period when they start out during which they are working extra hard to build up their customer base. It could be months, or more likely years, before they earn enough to live on their own and establish a regular client base. It also means they may have to deal with customers who have very different needs and expectations than they do. Let's say, for example, that you are a talented glass blower and get an inquiry from a chain of local high-end restaurants that are willing to place a large order that would really help you financially. But they may make demands about the size, color, consistency, or the cost of the glass products that are unappealing from the artist's point of view but make good sense from a business point of view. They may also want to negotiate cost, which is a business skill, not an artistic skill.

Marketing your art also means facing potential rejection, which can be demoralizing. Is your child prepared to hear the word *no* many more times than the word *yes*? Even established and famous actors get rejected for movie and TV roles if they are not a good fit for that particular project. And all the time spent on these myriad practical matters is time when they cannot be doing their art. Whether it is freelance writing, designing websites, or writing background music for commercials, artists can expect to spend as much as 50 percent of their time doing work other than actually creating their art. Do they have the fortitude to stick with these tasks so they can make room for the tasks they actually enjoy? Maybe an agent, a manager, a record label, or a studio can offload a lot of this work from an artist, but they then take a cut of the artist's earnings, sometimes a quite substantial one, to cover their costs. And those people are trying to make a living as well. They don't earn money unless the artist earns money, so just like the corporate client we mentioned earlier, they may be frequently pushing the artist to do projects to pay the bills, not because they truly fit with the artist's real passions. Big stars make enough to cover these professional costs and still make out well, but remember that we are encouraging your child to think through his future as if he became a modest success, not a big star. If the only way the economics work out is by being a big star, that is a highly risky and speculative approach to establishing a career. Either way, your child is not very likely to be successful as an independent artist without self-discipline and a strong work ethic. He should spend some time thinking about whether he has that level of commitment. Independent artists do not get paid unless they produce something, and it can feel very different to work as an artist in a mode where you must constantly produce or not eat.

To ease this pressure, a lot of independent artists have "day jobs" or side jobs as they are getting started so they can support themselves financially while they build up their client base or work toward a bigger break in their industry. This is a well-established tradition, and some artists take this approach through their entire life. We've all heard Oscar-winning actors talk about waiting tables or moving furniture, but this approach has its downsides. Working as a waiter, a house painter, a receptionist, or any other side job for that matter can leave you tired and wanting to tune out and take a break. Will your child have the discipline every day to carve out time in the early morning or after work in the evening to focus on art? How much of a side job will she need to pay her bills compared to how much effort it will take to break through as an artist? Can she carve out enough time for both? And if she decides she will paint houses for the rest of her life to support her artistic profession, what happens when she hurts her back or gets older and less interested in physical labor? How will she pay for health care or save for retirement?

We are not trying to discourage anyone from following their dreams. These are just realities that aspiring artists need to consider, and by considering them early on, they will be more likely to establish a realistic plan to navigate them. Sit down with a spreadsheet if you can and talk to your teen about what he might earn for his work, how much of it he would need to sell, and how much he could earn from side jobs that he imagines doing. Then see how this adds up, and compare it to the costs of renting a small apartment; paying for a small car, utilities, and groceries; and possibly paying off a student loan for art school or a specialized training program.

In particular, aspiring artists should look at a realistic time frame for how long it would take to reach the point of selling enough of their art to cover these costs. In many cases, it will not happen overnight. There will be time required to build up their work, market themselves, and eventually break through to a sustainable level, so talk to your child about realistic strategies for getting through these early and more difficult days.[1,2]

We understand that this exercise might seem totally alien to aspiring artists, as though it were almost disrespectful to imply that the money side of things would matter enough to pour cold water on the artistic passion with colorless math. These types of analyses are not what motivates kids to do what they love best. You may need to remind your teen that there are plenty of artists in midlife who wish they had paid more attention to numbers and contract details when they were younger and starting out. Artists who understand the business side of their industry are empowered to negotiate better, make more money, and ultimately have a better chance to be a full-time artist.

What can an actor, freelance writer, musician, or glass blower earn as an independent artist? The range is almost infinite. A quick Google search shows a single piece of blown glass made by Dale Chihuly, an iconic and ground-breaking glass sculptor, that is currently on sale for $28,000 (shipping not included). Another search on Etsy, an online marketplace for independent artists and makers, shows a lovely hand-blown glass lighting fixture for $225. According to *Billboard* magazine, a songwriter with at least one hit on the "Hot 100" could make anywhere from $100,000 to $2 million a year, while a cover band playing at smaller venues around the country can make $1,000 to $2,500 per appearance, which is then split four or five ways among the band after expenses. A good freelance writer could make between $200 and $500 for a blog post on a highly trafficked website. A freelance photographer can make anywhere from $15 to $50 per hour or charge between $2,500 and $10,000 to shoot a wedding. These are just general ranges that you can find with a simple online search, but clearly they vary widely depending on a number of factors. Here are some good resources for getting better information that may help you and your child draft a spreadsheet of potential earnings and think about ways to increase those earnings:

- *Blogs, online communities, and online databases.* Many artistic professions have blogs, online communities, and independent consultants who post articles about how to get ahead in their industry. Often these sites conduct surveys of their members or do research and report back on how much people are earning. Search for topics like "How much does a freelance photographer make?" or "How to earn more as a freelance writer" or "Tips for making money as a hip-hop producer" or "Average earnings for a freelance graphic designer." Often schools also have online resources that provide more in-depth information about careers and may feature profiles from people discussing their earnings or the challenges of working independently.
- *Marketplaces.* Look for online marketplaces where artists are selling their work so your child can get a better sense of how much similar artists are getting paid for their work. Sites like Etsy.com allow artists to sell their wares, so go there and search for products similar to what your child would sell. If your child produces music, go to Spotify and look up royalty rates. If your child wants to be a freelance mobile app developer, go to Upwork.com and try to find a top freelancer who does that to see what the going rate is. Search for terms like "freelance writer needed" or "looking for wedding photographer" or "music production gig" or "band seeks drummer." Often there are ads on sites like Craigslist.org that indicate pay rates for freelance services.

- *Talk to other artists.* See if your teen can reach out and connect with other artists in their field. You can search online for local artists in the area or potentially connect with artists in online communities. For example, a lot of music producers put their work up on Soundcloud.com. If your child follows a few up-and-coming producers who are not very famous yet, he could try to reach out through their public profile information on that site to see if the artist would do an informational interview, which is just a way for your child to learn more about how that artist earns a living.
- *Workshops.* One way a lot of artists earn extra money is teaching their craft to others. If you can afford it, sending your teen to participate in a workshop within her artistic field can be very valuable. It provides extra training and development of craft, and it creates a connection within the artistic community to someone who could be a mentor, provide information on how to better earn a living, or connect your teen to other members of that community who can provide the same benefits.

Ideally your teen would do research using all of these resources to get a more complete picture of their earnings potential. At the very least, kids can learn a lot more about their field and feel more confident in themselves if they have a strong commitment to their art.

Clearly there are pros and cons to both working independently and working full-time for a company. If your teen is serious about pursuing art as a career, it is worth talking through the differences and making an honest assessment of what jives well with his talents, personality, and lifestyle desires. As we discuss in chapter 11, there are ways to "try on" a career and learn more about it before making a big educational or career decision. Your teen can conduct informational interviews of freelance artists in her chosen field or possibly find an internship with a company that would expose her to the corporate side of working in her field. Contests are another great way to get some early exposure and feedback, and some companies like Disney even scout for talent through these.

Art Education

If your child wants to attend an art college or spend a couple of years at a specialized school to learn his craft, this can be a difficult family decision, especially if you as a parent help cover the cost. You may be skeptical that this expense will result in a successful career for your child and an ability to recover the costs. We hope that the topics we have already addressed will give you the basis for a wide-ranging discussion that can help you and your child develop a more realistic picture of their opportunities and the potentials risks. In addition, if your child wants to attend school to study art, we recommend that you work together to research the career placement success of that school's graduates and the typical amount of student loan debt for its graduates. What percentage of its graduates find immediate employment? What are the average earnings of its graduates within a year after graduation? How many of these graduates are still employed in their artistic field five years after graduation? How many of those students are still paying off student loan debt, and how much on average? Can the school put you in touch with successful alumni to help answer questions about their experience at that school? These colleges and art institutes may not be able to provide direct answers to those questions, but you should still try to find the answers online or by speaking to other students who attended if you can before making such an investment. Some degree programs have a very good reputation and track record of student success, and this will almost always be apparent by doing a good online search about the program and talking to former graduates.

When You Disagree

Let's say you and your teen spend a good amount of time talking through what we have discussed in this chapter, doing the research, and assembling a spreadsheet of numbers, but the results look unappealing from your perspective, possibly even unacceptable in your mind. Let's also suppose that your child insists that she will soldier on anyway because she cannot imagine doing anything else. How you handle this situation will be very personal to you, your child, and your unique situation. If your child is not going to college or art school after high school graduation but wants to start working as an artist immediately, there may be less financial risk for you as a parent (or maybe not if you feel obligated to support your son or daughter), but you will still obviously be concerned about his future financial stability.

A strategy that may be helpful would be to see if you can get your teen to think about setting some personal milestones, especially around artistic output. For example, let's say that together in your research, you learned that a successful freelance writer in your son's area of interest tends to produce somewhere around three articles a week of at least one thousand words per article. You could then ask him how long he thinks it would take him to reach the point of producing that much output every week, even if it was not all work for which he got paid. Perhaps you could get him to agree that if he achieves a milestone like that within a certain time frame, then he has a much better chance of being successful. If he does not achieve such a milestone, it could be worth further discussion about revisiting alternative career strategies.

A Final Thought

One last topic you may want to discuss with your teen is whether she could pursue her artistic interests as a side passion while also working full-time in a well-paying profession that is not in the arts. This may seem like giving up on a dream, but in some ways, it could be the best of both worlds. If she is really interested in art as its own reward and is not obsessed with fame or fortune, then she might be able to get all the personal benefits of practicing her art part-time while getting the financial benefits and stability of a more practical full-time career.

There is some freedom in this approach. She could pursue art for the love of it and put her work out there without the fear that comes from needing that work to pay bills. Each of us has met many people from all walks of life at work, at church, or in social situations who have wonderful artistic pursuits on the side of a successful full-time career in a nonartistic field. The biggest key to making this work is having the self-discipline to regularly carve out time to practice and create. Artists can accomplish a tremendous amount by working consistently every day, even if only for an hour at a time. And this does not have to mean an end to any long-term aspiration of producing a major work. Andy Weir, author of *The Martian*, wrote his breakout novel as a series of online posts while working full-time as a computer programmer, so it does happen.

We hope that we have provided a wide range of topics to help focus your discussions with your teen about pursuing artistic interests, whether it is through the challenge of building a career as an independent artist, working full-time for a company, or just hold onto a lifelong passion for creating art while building a career in another field.

Sample Earnings Outlook

Following is a sample of 2015 median annual earnings for various jobs in the artistic and creative professions according to the Bureau of Labor Statistics:

- Graphic designer: $46,900
- Interior designer: $48,840
- Music composer: $50,110
- Multimedia artist/animator: $63,970
- Fashion designer: $63,670
- Craftsman/fine artist: $45,080
- Photographer: $31,710
- Video editor: $55,740
- Writer/author: $60,250
- Actor: $18.80 per hour ($39,104 annually for those who work forty hours per week)

For wage information on other careers in the field not listed here, and for more detailed local wage information or job prospects, we recommend using the online Occupational Outlook Handbook provided free by the Bureau of Labor Statistics at https://www.bls.gov/ooh/home.htm.

Keep in mind that we are showing median pay, so some people in these roles may earn substantially less and others may earn substantially more. Generally pay is higher in locations where the cost of living is higher and in fields that are growing more rapidly or require more specialization and experience. In addition to using the *Occupational Outlook Handbook* website, we recommend that your son or daughter conduct an Internet search using terms like "future job prospects for [career name]" to get the most current outlook on industry growth potential.

9

Should You Consider a Career in Law or Criminal Justice?

One of the most eye-opening experiences of my (Shaun's) life was sitting for five weeks on a District of Columbia grand jury, hearing testimony for over fifty felony cases, including fifteen homicides. It was depressing and harrowing, yet it provided a rare look inside the criminal justice system of a major urban area. I learned that most prosecutors work weekends to keep up with their never-ending caseloads and that murder cases can drag on for years before an indictment, much less an actual trial. I sat aghast as a convicted murderer described how his entire neighborhood used technology like Facebook to quickly spread the word that he was testifying against another member of the neighborhood, so he would now be marked for death if he ever returned. I learned that most cases depend on old-fashioned eyewitness accounts, grainy video camera footage without magical zoom-in capabilities, and basic detective work, not ingenious crime scene investigators or eccentric computer hackers. I learned that it can take months to get fingerprint or DNA results and the important difference between concepts like "probable cause" and "beyond a reasonable doubt." And I witnessed an endless cycle of crime poisoning a community with heartbreaking poverty, unemployment, incarceration, absent parents, drugs, and fear. Serving on a jury isn't like it's made out to be in the movies.

Few other career fields capture the public imagination more than law and criminal justice. Every month it seems that there is a new television series featuring a troubled but clever detective, a scrappy prosecutor, an elusive criminal, a brilliant CSI tech, or an irritated judge fed up with yet another objection. These tropes never seem to get old, and even if they do, we consume them anyway like good comfort food. But they may also do a disservice by misleading young people who are considering a career in law or criminal justice.

In this chapter we discuss some of the differences between the myths and realities of these career fields and expose you and your teen to a broader world of opportunities than what you may have seen on TV and in the movies. We look at criminal justice first, both with respect to work as a lawyer and other careers such as police officer, corrections officer, detective, or crime scene investigator. Then we discuss law as a career outside criminal justice, such as corporate, environmental, and family law.

Criminal Justice

There are many pathways into a criminal justice career and many ways to move from one part of the field to the other, so your teen does not need to have everything figured out ahead of time before choosing an entry point. A police officer can become a detective, go back to school and get a law degree, or move into corporate security. A military police officer can transition to civilian law enforcement and join a SWAT team. A prosecutor can become a private defense attorney, go to work for a large law firm, or run for public office. And all of these individuals could take a lot of their skills and use them to transition into civilian careers in business or self-employment.

Police and Investigative Work

Most entry-level careers in policing or corrections require some education beyond high school such as a certificate program, an associate degree, or graduation from a police department's law enforcement academy. A certificate program covers topics such as basic criminology, the laws and procedures of the criminal justice system, and the foundations of corrections practices and procedures. A two-year associate degree program also covers a more detailed survey of various types of crime, policing strategy and techniques, and the basics of handling a crime scene.

Those who complete a certificate or associate degree program or a law enforcement academy can then apply for a specific policing or corrections position and most likely need to pass a law enforcement exam. If they have done well in their studies, the exam should be very manageable with a bit of preparation. They also need to pass a physical exam, which may require them to do things like simulate running after a suspect on foot for seventy-five yards, complete push-ups and sit-ups in a certain amount of time, and complete a longer endurance run within a specific time limit. We hope this is obvious, but prior to being offered a law enforcement job, your child will also be subject to comprehensive criminal background checks and a drug test.

Kids who are thinking about police or investigative work but want a wider range of options can complete a bachelor's degree program, which will add subjects such as police ethics, emergency management, and more advanced study of police methods like intelligence gathering. Entry-level federal jobs in Homeland Security such as a border patrol agent, FBI agent, CIA analyst, or specialized government policing jobs such as wildlife and game officer require a minimum of a bachelor's degree. Students who cannot afford a bachelor's degree program or want to get to work sooner can always start with an associate degree, work for a few years, and then go back to earn their bachelor's degree. Having work experience can give them an advantage in job hunting once they complete their four-year degree. However, it's important to spend some time investigating specific bachelor's degree programs and making sure that the credits from the associate degree program they select are guaranteed to transfer to the bachelor's degree programs they might choose later. (We discuss this more in chapter 14.)

Your teen might be surprised to learn that there are other degree types besides criminal justice that can lead to an interesting career in law enforcement. Two of the most important areas in law enforcement with promising growth opportunities are accounting and information technology. Financial crime and cybercrime have grown as the finance industry has become more complex and networked computer systems have become central to almost every business, so these skills are in high demand and will likely lead to better pay than more traditional policing and investigator roles. Kids who have an interest in both law enforcement and business or law enforcement and computer technology could get a bachelor's degree in accounting or information technology and be well positioned for either career path. They could also try taking a few classes in criminal justice and then either do a double major or select their chosen field a bit later in college.

There are some common misconceptions about police work that you can discuss with your teen. First, success as a police officer is not all about physical strength or facing down danger. Day-to-day police work involves much more than chasing bad guys; in fact, most police officers never have to use deadly force during their entire career. Police work requires a lot of mental and social/emotional attributes like the ability to communicate well with members of the community, effective teamwork with other officers and detectives, a solid knowledge of laws and regulations, and the patience to follow procedure and provide complete, well-written reports. There are specialized teams that do more dramatic work such as conducting raids or responding to hostage situations, but these are a small part of a much larger police force, and entry into these teams is based on prior work experience or military experience that naturally screens out anyone not well suited to those tasks. Another misconception is that police work is primarily a male occupation or that female police officers have only limited roles. Women have just as many opportunities as men within both police work and corrections, including everything from the traditional patrol officer or detective, to specialized roles that require more sensitivity, such as domestic violence or sexual abuse investigators.

Detectives

What if your child dreams of being a homicide detective, carefully following clues, interrogating suspects, and getting bad guys off the streets? There are a few things to consider. First, these detectives need to be part of a larger police force, usually in an urban area, so there are enough homicide detective positions available to have a reasonable chance at earning one. Second, the typical pathway to homicide detective is by spending at least several years as a patrol officer and likely much more than that. It could be ten years before these officers finally get a detective position, and it's not usually homicide at first. They might have to serve as a detective on burglary, robbery, assault, sex offense, drug, or auto theft cases before getting a rotation into homicide. Also, homicide is generally the most coveted detective position, so a great track record as a patrol officer, which is as much about teamwork, thoroughness, and attitude as it is about how many arrests made or the ability to run down a fast suspect on foot, helps. Even for those who turn out to have exceptional investigative talents, the reality of job assignments in a police department is not much different from the reality within many other career fields. Office politics, personality, and favoritism can trump job performance when it comes time to appoint a new homicide detective. If this is truly your teen's dream, she should try to find a detective or two for informational interviewing, as we discuss in chapter 10, and get some advice on the best way to conduct a patrol officer career to position herself for promotion to detective, in addition to learning more about the realities of the job.

In some communities, fluency in languages other than English could increase the likelihood of making homicide detective and accelerate the time line. Your teen should understand that homicide detective work is not like what is typically portrayed on television. Prosecutors refer to this as the "CSI effect," which leads many jury members to expect a lot of forensic evidence in every murder case. The reality in many murder cases is that there may be a lot of evidence showing that someone was murdered but very little to prove beyond a reasonable doubt who did it. Detectives can spend endless hours following up on old-fashioned leads like eyewitnesses, only to discover that they refuse to talk or give conflicting accounts. Forensic evidence may often be enough to put a suspect near a murder scene or establish a motive, but not enough for conviction, and it can sometimes take up to six months to get fingerprint or DNA evidence returned from a lab.

Detective work is more likely to involve conversations with many people, tedious hours of searching through phone records, and writing reports for prosecutors than having a Netflix-worthy lightning bolt of intuition. Finally, television often gives the impression that detectives get to spend all their time diligently working through a single case. In fact, being a detective is like a lot of other jobs where you get a bunch of projects piled on your plate and your boss is breathing down your neck to get them done. Detectives are measured by their productivity in closing cases and they are busy working multiple cases at once.

Crime Scene Investigation and Forensics

Crime scene investigation (CSI) and forensic science have experienced an increase in popularity, fueled by the proliferation of television shows and movies featuring brainy technicians and scientists who find the big break to solve a case. Crime scene investigators are technicians who specialize in carefully collecting evidence from a crime scene, whereas forensic scientists typically work in a laboratory setting and conduct their work after evidence has been collected.

Preparation for crime scene technician and investigator jobs does not require intensive science training. CSI education is mostly learning about collection techniques, procedures for gathering and storing evidence, and general criminal justice topics. Some law enforcement academies provide specialized CSI training for entry-level positions, so the path can be from high school, to the police academy, and into a CSI tech job. There are also one-year CSI certificate programs as well as associate and bachelor's degree programs that offer CSI specializations, which can lead to higher-paying CSI roles. Exceptional students in a four-year degree program can apply for CSI internships at places like the CIA, the Secret Service, and the Federal Law Enforcement Center, which provide elite-level training.

Teens who are more interested in laboratory and scientific work should explore forensic science, which involves conducting tests on evidence after it has already been removed from the crime scene. Becoming a forensic scientist likely requires a four-year degree in a subject like biology, chemistry, toxicology, pharmacology, or physics (see chapter 4 for more on STEM degrees). Because of how frequently these careers are portrayed on television, we strongly suggest that your teen try to speak with someone practicing as a CSI or forensic scientist to get a better sense of the actual experience and responsibilities. A common misconception is that a CSI or forensic scientist is involved in the whole criminal investigation, possibly even interrogating suspects, making arrests, or doing other police work. In reality, these roles are limited to specific technical aspects of the case, while other investigators do the rest of the detective work. Forensic science, for example, can involve long hours of tedious laboratory work, which is more akin to quiet scientific research under fluorescent lights and not a fast-paced investigation with a friendly team of investigators popping by to chat.

Another common TV portrayal is that forensic work provides rapid results that identify the exact person responsible for the crime along with a name, photo, and address where the person can be arrested immediately. In reality, lab results can take days or months depending on the urgency or type of case. Also, not all criminals' fingerprints or DNA are in a database, and many cases may have either too little forensic evidence or contaminated evidence that is not conclusive enough to remove reasonable doubt. Forensic scientists are also conducting so many tests on a regular basis that they often do not even learn the final outcome of a case, so they can feel very disconnected from the thrill of justice that might have originally drawn them to the field. That is not to say there is nothing exciting about this work. In one of Shaun's grand jury cases, a federal laboratory was going to recreate an entire apartment bedroom and set it on fire to determine whether a murder was the result of an arson or a physical assault. There is no doubt that that is a pretty cool job. As a general rule, though, practitioners are a lot more likely to get that kind of work as they increase their level of education (a bachelor's or master's degree) and work experience.

Criminal Law

All of the police work, detective investigations, CSI evidence collection, and forensic testing ultimately go nowhere without a prosecutor, a government attorney who must establish probable cause to indict a suspect and then either cut a deal with the defendant or ultimately present the case in front of a jury if it goes to trial and recommend a sentence if the defendant is convicted. Young people are often drawn to become prosecutors out of a desire to see justice done or in some cases as a path to become a judge or start a political career. On the other side of the case is the defense attorney, sometimes an overworked public defender and sometimes a private attorney (or many attorneys, depending on the case). People are often drawn to these defense roles for altruistic reasons, but they can also be appealing because certain kinds of defense attorneys can earn very large amounts of money. Corporate and white-collar criminal defense attorneys or litigators leading class action lawsuits against major corporations can earn millions, but despite what you see on television, defending murderers, drug dealers, and violent criminals is not typically a pathway to earning a lot of money.

Whether you are on the side of the government or working for the defense, there will be no getting around having a law degree. That means your child will need to earn a bachelor's degree from a four-year college, then take the LSAT (Harvard Law School now also accepts the GRE), and apply to law school. The field of law in general has gone through some significant changes recently, and law school enrollment is down due to fewer job opportunities overall than in decades past. There is a still a high bar, however, for admission to a top-quality law school, and your child will be competing against some of the most academically successful students from top liberal arts colleges and universities. Once your child completes law school and receives the JD degree, she will have to pass the bar exam for the state in which she intends to practice. In many cases, recent law school graduates can find a job that will allow them to start immediately and provide a probationary period during which they study for and pass the bar exam. It is an extensive and intense exam.

High-profile positions such as a homicide prosecutor in a big city or a federal white-collar crime prosecutor are highly competitive. The best and brightest out of law school are competing for these positions, so your child should expect to work extremely hard in school to achieve this goal. Prosecutors can earn good salaries, but nothing even close to those of high-end corporate attorneys, so this is not a career typically pursued for the money. The workload is often grueling, and these attorneys will be under intense public scrutiny. For this reason, many people go into this career with an assumption that they will put in a certain amount of time, establish their reputation, and then use their experience as a launch pad to other legal careers that are more lucrative (corporate) or have a better work/life balance (judge), or to a political career (legislator). All of these transitions depend on a strong work ethic, a good personal reputation, and a high level of achievement.

If your child ultimately aspires to be a judge, this will typically be a long road. Aspiring judges must first acquire experience practicing as a lawyer and build a good reputation. Then they need to submit their name to a judicial nominating commission or be recommended by someone in a prominent political position. Those who are successful in getting appointed then typically undergo some additional training provided by the state or federal government and serve as a judge for a specified term. Not all judicial appointments are permanent. Many expire after a certain period and judges must be reappointed or elected.

Noncriminal Law

Up to this point we have focused primarily on studying and practicing law in the context of criminal justice. However, there are many other ways to practice law—for example:

- Maritime law (shipping, navigation)
- Business law (contracts, litigation, mergers, tax, bankruptcy, international)
- Environmental law (regulatory compliance, litigation)
- Health care law (regulatory compliance, medical malpractice)
- Labor law (unions, discrimination, compensation)
- Intellectual property law (trademarks, copyrights, patents)
- Estate law (wills and trusts)
- Entertainment law (contracts, copyrights)
- Family law (divorce, custody, adoption)

Just like criminal justice law fields, all of these require completing a bachelor's degree at a four-year college, applying to law school, completing a law degree, and passing an intensive bar exam. Even if your child starts law school with the intent to practice criminal law, she can always change her mind and practice many other forms of law if criminal justice is not as appealing as she thought it would be. Those who pass the bar exam can practice any kind of law with their degree.

Law schools offer specializations or elective course work in many of these areas; other areas may require that lawyers develop expertise mostly on the job. If your child also has a strong interest in business or science and technology, there are excellent opportunities to combine academic study in these fields with a law degree to increase specialization and pursue jobs that may be in higher demand and offer greater pay. Patent law, for example, requires an inventor to prove that an invention is worthy of a patent on both legal and technical grounds, so a patent lawyer must have an excellent knowledge of the law but also the technical skills to understand the invention and assist the inventor with creating an adequate description for the U.S. Patent and Trade Office reviewers. Your child could combine an undergraduate degree in physics or computer science, for example, with a law degree and be well positioned to enter patent law. For students interested in business and law, specialized dual-degree programs allow a student to

complete a JD and earn an MBA within a shorter period of time than if each
was pursued separately. This provides excellent career flexibility since the
business knowledge makes these students more valuable as corporate attorneys
and increases the likelihood they can move from corporate law into business
leadership positions like a CEO. There are plenty of examples in business of
CEOs or senior corporate executives who started out as corporate lawyers.

Salaries for lawyers are generally good on average compared to other
career fields and can be exceptionally high for those who work in specialized
fields or are hired by the most prestigious private law firms or government
lobbying firms.

Job prospects for entry-level positions, though, took a significant hit
during the Great Recession and have not rebounded as quickly as some other
career fields. For this reason, law school attendance is down from where it was
a decade ago, and there are more new graduates with law degrees who have
struggled to find entry-level positions. Job availability in some areas also
depends heavily on government changes. The current presidential administration, for example, is pushing heavily to relax a lot of environmental
regulation, which may lessen the need for corporations to retain environmental law expertise and slow demand for hiring in that field. The new
administration is also dramatically changing the landscape for immigration,
which can affect businesses as much as individuals, so immigration law may
experience rapid growth.

Another trend affecting demand for legal services is computer automation and artificial intelligence. As we mentioned in chapter 7 on business
careers, JPMorgan recently announced the rollout of new artificial intelligence software to interpret and review commercial loan agreements. This
software can now do what loan officers and lawyers spent over 360,000 hours
a year doing for JPMorgan previously. A fair amount of low-level legal work
requires legal knowledge but does not require much advanced skill. If a job
primarily involves being trained to understand a set of legal rules and then
repeatedly using those rules to review, edit, or flag some issue in a written
contract, computers can likely take over that task. In the coming decades,
corporations and computer scientists will continue to collaborate on ways to
automate these routine jobs.

For these reasons, it's important for your child to think about the kinds of
knowledge and skills that will remain valuable over the long run in a legal
career. This includes areas such as business skills, technology skills, scientific

knowledge, and foreign languages. It also includes entrepreneurship. Many people have heard of Herb Kelleher, the charismatic CEO and cofounder of Southwest Airlines, the most consistently profitable airline in history. What they may not know is that Herb started out as a lawyer helping other companies incorporate, and the original founder of Southwest Airlines had approached him to help incorporate the new airline. Herb continued to keep his private law practice open for several years until finally being asked to take over as full-time CEO of Southwest.

Practicing law takes years of hard work and self-discipline, and it requires a keen analytical mind. These are all attributes of a successful entrepreneur and having legal expertise can be an invaluable asset and a money-saver for those who go into business for themselves. If your child is interested in both law and entrepreneurship, we strongly suggest you read chapter 7 on business.

Law School

About two hundred law schools in the United States are approved by the American Bar Association to confer a JD degree. Unlike undergraduate college, where there are thousands of options, the differences in quality and reputation of a law school can have a greater impact on career opportunities. Graduates from the top fifteen or so law schools are more likely to find entry-level employment at elite law firms or in highly coveted state and federal clerkships. And given the recent downturn in entry-level positions for law school graduates, a law degree from a more reputable law school could provide a material advantage. That does not mean that if your child attends a lower-ranked law school she will have trouble finding a job, but it does mean that she may want to give this more consideration than when choosing an undergraduate college. It also means that your child should think carefully about selecting an undergraduate college experience that is challenging but achievable.

No specific kind of undergraduate major is required to prepare for law school. Some four-year colleges offer a legal studies or prelaw degree, but there is no evidence that these majors or a criminal justice major provide any advantage when applying to law school. As your teen contemplates what he will study, he should consider a major that will be interesting enough to motivate him to study hard and get excellent grades. Another consideration is a major that will challenge him to develop critical thinking skills and an ability to articulate and defend strong intellectual arguments. Majors that require a lot of reading, writing, and critical argument will likely be more helpful. Common choices are English, history, political science, economics, journalism, philosophy, and business.

Before we finish the topic of law school, it is worth noting a couple of things that can be disconcerting to young people who have worked hard to reach law school, especially if they are focused on criminal justice. First, law is *amoral*. That means that the law is a set of agreed-on rules written by legislators and interpreted by judges, not a moral code. Morality and legality are two different concepts. Whether someone is prosecuted and convicted of a crime is not about our personal moral sense of right and wrong. It is about whether the words we have agreed on as law can be interpreted clearly to mean that a person should legally be prosecuted. This can be jarring to those who entered law school inspired by moral conviction. Sometimes bad people get away with their crimes because laws are poorly written, incomplete, or extremely specific in their conditions for guilt. Second, law school does not teach many of the practical skills of a working lawyer. Much of what law students study is theoretical in nature. The skills for day-to-day work in law, such as filing briefs, drafting contracts, deciding whether to prosecute, cross-examining witnesses, and making closing arguments to a jury, are usually learned on the job. Some large corporate law firms have established their own internal education programs to teach their newly hired associates how to do real-world legal work. Of course, there are other career fields where a lot of knowledge comes from on-the-job experience, but it's helpful if those who aspire to a legal career go in with their eyes open about it because it requires an intense amount of academic preparation (and expense) only to show up the first day of your job and discover that they don't know a lot about how to actually do the practical work.

The men and women working in criminal justice today are some of the most hard-working and dedicated public servants in our society. Criminal justice or law careers can be fulfilling and sometimes provide surprising opportunities to directly improve the lives of others. Law provides much of the foundation of our democratic society and our free-market economy and will always be an important career that is in demand. We hope that by discussing the topics we have covered in this chapter, you can give your child a better chance at finding the kind of law or criminal justice career that will be both fulfilling personally and meet his financial goals in life.

Sample Earnings Outlook

Following is a sample of 2015 median annual earnings for various jobs in criminal justice and law according to the Bureau of Labor Statistics:

- Paralegal: $48,810
- Lawyer: $115,820
- Judge: $109, 010
- Correctional officer: $40,580
- Police officer/detective: $60,270
- Security guard: $24,680

For wage information on other careers in the field not listed here, and for more detailed local wage information or job prospects, we recommend using the online *Occupational Outlook Handbook* provided free by the Bureau of Labor Statistics at https://www.bls.gov/ooh/home.htm.

Keep in mind that we are showing median pay, so some people in these roles may earn substantially less and others may earn substantially more. Generally pay is higher in locations where the cost of living is higher and in fields that are growing more rapidly or that require more specialization and experience. In addition to using the Occupational Outlook Handbook website, we recommend that your child conduct an Internet search using terms like "future job prospects for [career name]," to get the most current outlook on industry growth potential.

PART III

How Will You Get to Where You Want to Go?

10

How Can You Try On Your Career Interests?

I (Shaun) changed my major in college three times. I started in physics, then changed to electrical engineering, and finally landed in economics. Even then I wasn't entirely sure that was right for me, as he also really liked Asian languages and Asian history, but he was running out of time to change my mind and needed to make a decision and finish his degree. According to data from the U.S. Department of Education, about 80 percent of college students change their major at least once. The reason that young people are so likely to change their future educational and career interests is that they lack experience. We cannot truly know something until we try it. A fascination with history is one thing. Reading three books a week and writing five papers a semester is entirely different. Similarly, a fondness for babysitting and helping children is quite different from managing a classroom of twenty-five third graders, some of whom have significant learning differences, and making sure they are all on track to pass a test that measures Common Core Standards for math.

This sounds obvious, but it is remarkable how frequently we make educational and career decisions based on gut instinct or following the path of least resistance instead of actively trying to get some experience to better inform ourselves, even as adults. In this chapter we give you a set of strategies to discuss with your child about how he or she can try on career interests before committing too deeply to an extensive education or a career in that field. Our hope is that these strategies can be valuable for your teen's whole life, not just the beginning of his or her career.

Before discussing these strategies, we want to emphasize a couple of points. First, we don't believe that a career is completely dependent on your degree. Throughout this book, we note that a certain type of education or degree can be perfectly fine preparation for careers in a wide range of fields, even those outside the general category. A biology major can become a financial analyst, and a journalism major can become a mobile app developer. More than ever before, talent trumps pedigree, and if you have any kind of bachelor's degree at all, that's an indication to potential employers that you are likely to be intelligent, motivated, and capable of working hard. Second, no matter what your experience is, there is no way to have your life all mapped out ahead of time. What would be the fun in that? There may come a time in a person's life when it could be very impractical to become a neurosurgeon or fly jets for the Navy, but for most people, many career pathways could lead to fulfillment and it's probably not too late to try at least one of these. These two common misconceptions, that your degree limits your career choices and that it is too late to try something new once you pick a certain path, can create unnecessary stress and keep us from exploring fulfilling pathways in the future. With that in mind, let's help your teen learn more about herself and make more informed choices about her future.

We are assuming that if you are reading this chapter, your son or daughter already has some general or specific interests in a career direction. If not, it's okay; there is no reason to worry. There are plenty of students entering college with a major of "undecided" who ultimately select a major after their freshman year. But if your child wants to begin exploring future careers and does not have any specific thoughts, there are a variety of resources to discover more about themselves and explore career fields to get a couple of initial starting points based on their interests and strengths. We discuss helpful ways to approach this a lot more in the first few chapters of this book if you have not already read them.

Informational Interviewing

One of the most useful ways to try on a career is through informational interviewing—essentially connecting with people in a specific career field and spending some informal time with them to ask questions, establish a relationship, and learn more about that career from people who do it. There are websites that will let you read a lot about specific careers and even watch video interviews of people talking about their daily experience in that career, but there is no substitute for being able to talk to someone in person. Magazine articles and online resources don't always capture the firsthand realities that you might pick up through a more candid conversation, where you can speak off the record and watch someone's facial expressions.

Another benefit of informational interviewing is to get a better understanding of how to prepare for a specific career field and learn the typical pathway into an entry-level job. This can help your teen make better decisions about where to attend college or what major to select and give her ideas for how to better position herself for a job opportunity when she is ready to apply.[1]

Finally, informational interviewing can be a great way for your child to start forming professional relationships within a chosen career field. Because it is a low-key conversation without pressuring anyone for a job, kids have a good opportunity to develop a relationship that could allow them to reach out again in the future for advice, mentoring, or perhaps a referral to someone else in the field who may be looking to fill a job opening. We now explore the basic steps of information interviewing.

Step 1: Find People to Interview

Once your teen has some specific interests, the first step is to try to connect with people practicing in that career field. This may be a daunting prospect for teenagers without much experience in the world, but their youth can also be an advantage. Some adults may feel compelled to help a young person and flattered that they have been asked for advice. And since they are not going to be asked for an actual job, there is less pressure or concern than if they are being approached by an adult. Some people may be too busy or uninterested in helping but still feel compelled to refer your child to a peer or colleague who has more interest and time. There can be many direct or indirect sources for people to interview, and your son or daughter should try all of them to generate as many potential resources as possible.

First, you and your teen should try to think of family members, friends of family members, friends of your child's teachers, or colleagues at your office who may know someone in a particular career. Second, you can use the Internet to research professional associations that may list people, or you could try to reach out using a site like LinkedIn. If you as a parent have a LinkedIn account and have a network established on LinkedIn, it is possible to pay for a premium account that allows you to directly send email to your second-degree contacts (contacts of your direct contacts), but this may be worth it only if you have a decent sized network already. You would be surprised how quickly you might be able to find someone working in a career field if you ask a lot of different people and you make it clear that you are just looking for information about a career field for your teenager, and are not seeking a job.

Step 2: Prepare

Your teen should prepare a list of questions ahead of time (see Step 6) and have a brief personal introduction (no more than thirty seconds) that is just a quick overview of who he is and why he is seeking an informational interview. Before arriving for the interview, he should also try to search for information on the interviewee or his or her employer. Having this background information will make your teen better prepared for the interview and can create a good impression on the interviewee, who will see that this young person is serious about this career and be more willing to help in the future.

Step 3: Reach Out

After your teen has developed a list of potential contacts, it is time to ask for a meeting or phone call. She can reach out by phone or email. If she chooses to call, she should not assume she can have a conversation during that first phone call and should not assume the person will say yes. However, she should be ready with questions in case the contact says that he would prefer to talk during the initial outreach. We offer suggestions later in this chapter for a sample phone introduction and email introduction.

Your teen should always mention how she found out about the person she wants to interview, especially if it was a personal connection from a friend or family member. Also, make sure she knows that it's normal for people to say no to requests like this and should not take a refusal personally. Even people who have interest in talking to your child may simply not have the time. Rejection is a natural part of life, so this is an opportunity for your child to learn that she can handle it and keep moving toward their goal through persistence.

Step 4: Conduct the Interview

If your teen is meeting in person, make sure he dresses appropriately, similar to how he might dress for a job interview, and make sure he arrives on time. If your child is conducting the interview by phone, he should ask again to make sure it is a good time to talk.

To begin the conversation, your child should quickly remind the interviewee who he is and what he hopes to accomplish with the conversation. If your child is in high school, it may not be necessary to remind the person that he is not asking for a job, but it can be helpful to reiterate that he is calling to learn, not to ask for a job or job referral (this is especially important if your child is in college). That can always come later if a good relationship is established.

Your child should try to listen more than he talks and be prepared to keep the conversation moving with a list of questions. It can be helpful to take a few notes, but we suggest he limits notes to the key points he wants to remember later or maybe something interesting he wants to research more. Taking excessive notes can sap the energy from a conversation and annoy the interviewee. Your child should spend most of his energy listening and engaging in a free-flowing and candid discussion for the best results.

Remember that this is as much an opportunity to establish a relationship as it is to get information. It is important to stay within the agreed-on time range for the discussion and offer to end the conversation when that time arrives. As the conversation wraps up, your child can ask if it is okay to reach out again with any follow-up questions and also ask if there is anyone else with whom the interviewee thinks he should speak.

Step 5: Post-interview Follow-up

After the interview, your teen should take some time to think about what she learned and maybe add to her notes for future reference. It can be very helpful for her to discuss what she learned with you. She should also follow up with a thank-you note as soon as possible—no more than a couple of days. If she had a positive conversation and thinks she made a good connection, she should consider sending a follow-up note to that person if she decides to pursue that career field, letting the person know what she is up to so they can stay in touch.

Step 6: Evaluation

Once your child has completed a few informational interviews, he should sit down and give some thought to what he learned and then discuss it with you. Here are some helpful questions you can ask your child to get him thinking in a useful way:

- How did you feel at the end of it? Did you feel energized, indifferent, or disappointed?
- Can you imagine being the person you interviewed? Would that excite you? If not, why?
- Was the information you learned about the career different from what you had imagined it would be like? If yes, how so?
- Did the actual daily work sound engaging to you? Do you think that type of work makes sense for your personality and strengths?
- What preparation is needed for this job? Is it a lot of learning in school or more about on-the-job experience, or both? Do you think you would be okay with that?

Sample Phone Introduction

This introduction is for a cold call to someone without a personal referral:

Hi, my name is Pat Smith, and I'm a senior at Robert Johnson High School. I'm trying to find people to interview about criminal justice careers, and I was wondering if I could have just a minute of your time to see if we could schedule a conversation?

If this was a personal referral from a friend or family member, make sure to include that:

> *Hi, my name is Pat Smith, and I'm a senior at Robert Johnson High School. I'm trying to find people to interview about criminal justice careers and my civics teacher, Mr. Burke, said he thought you might be able to offer a helpful perspective. I was wondering if I could have just a minute of your time to see if we could schedule a conversation.*

If the person says yes:

> *Could we schedule maybe thirty to forty-five minutes of time to talk sometime this week or next? I would be happy to buy you a cup of coffee, or we could talk on the phone.*

If the person asks for more information about what the teenager is trying to accomplish:

> *I'm interested in learning what a career in criminal justice is actually like in the real world, so I can figure out if it would be a good fit for me, and maybe also get some ideas about the best way to prepare myself.*

If the person says he doesn't have time to help out but still seems nice, try asking for another referral:

> *Sure, I understand. Is there anyone else you know who might be interested in speaking with me?*

If the person seems annoyed by the call or says no without being very friendly about it:

> *Okay. I understand. Thank you for your time and have a good day.*

Sample Email Introduction

> *Kathy, my name is Pat Smith, and I'm a senior at Robert Johnson High School. I'm trying to find people to interview about criminal justice careers, and I was wondering if you would be willing to speak with me. I'm very interested in criminal justice careers and I want to learn as much as I can about the field. My civics teacher, Mr. Burke, said that*

he thought you might be able to offer a helpful perspective. If that sounds okay with you, could we schedule maybe thirty minutes of time to talk sometime this week or next? I would be happy to buy you a cup of coffee, or we could talk on the phone. Also, if there is anyone else you think I should speak with, please let me know. Thank you for your time, and I look forward to hearing from you.

Sincerely,

Pat

Informational Interview Questions

As you can see from the list that follows, there are a lot of questions your teen could ask someone about a career, but you should spend some time helping her to strategize about the questions that matter most for her. Maybe she has some doubts about a certain aspect. Maybe you are concerned that she is being unrealistic about something in particular. It's worth prioritizing the list in case she runs out of time during the interview.

- What do you spend most of your time doing?
- What is a typical work week like for you?
- What do you like most about your job?
- What do you like least about it?
- What are the most challenging parts of your job?
- What are the most rewarding parts of your job?
- Are there any common misconceptions that people have about what you do?
- Do you work alone or spend a lot of time working with others?
- How does your position fit within your overall organization/company?
- Where do you plan to go next with your career?
- What kind of work/life balance do you have?
- Do you get to keep learning new things?
- Do you travel or go to conferences?
- Do you feel like this is a financially rewarding career field?
- Are there good opportunities to advance in terms of responsibility and pay?
- What types of accomplishments are highly valued and rewarded in this career?
- What got you interested in this career?

- How did you get started?
- Is there a typical path to entering this field? What kind of educational background do entry-level employees have in this field?
- What did you study in college, and was that very relevant to your career?
- What are the educational or training requirements for this career?
- Are there certain skills or abilities that make a person more likely to succeed in this career?
- Are there other related career fields that you think I should consider?
- If you could start over, would you choose the same career path? Would you do anything differently?
- Are there any online resources or trade journals that I should explore to learn more about this career field?
- Are there any big changes or trends going on that will affect this career field?
- What do you think are the best ways to find a good position in this field once I complete my education/training?
- Is there any reason you would not encourage someone to pursue this career path?
- How long do people typically stay in this career? Do they often move on to a certain type of career after this?
- Are there other people with whom you think I should speak?

Job Shadowing

Job shadowing is similar to informational interviewing but involves actually spending a day (or part of a day) on the job with a person, following her around as a "shadow," observing her work, and asking questions when appropriate. Job shadowing is more difficult to arrange than an informational interview, but has some advantages. Your teen can watch as someone conducts a job and observe things that a person might not think to share during an interview. Watching a person in action may also prompt questions that your teen had not originally imagined ahead of time. Finally, she can observe other intangibles such as what kind of atmosphere surrounds the job. Is it quiet or lively? Is the host around a lot of people or often alone? Does the host spend most of her day sitting at a desk or get to move around a lot? What are the rest of the people like who work around the person your teen is shadowing? Also, during the day, your teen may bump into other people in the same organization who can also answer questions and provide another perspective.

Your teen should approach job shadowing in a similar way to the informational interview in terms of how to find the opportunities, to reach out, and to articulate the kind of information she seeks during the experience. Some industries may have well-established practices of offering job shadow opportunities to high school students, and your child's school may have relationships with local employers where students make connections every year. These tend to be career fields where the job activities are very tangible and visible, such as medicine, technology, manufacturing, clinical work, and criminal justice, but there is no specific rule about which type of job is appropriate for a job shadow, so there is no harm in your child's reaching out to someone and asking if a job shadow would be feasible. Your teen can always ask for an informational interview if job shadowing is not an option.

Here is some basic etiquette that we recommend you review with your teen before the shadow experience:

- Dress appropriately. It's fine to ask the shadow host what would be appropriate to wear ahead of time. Remove a hat before entering the premises.
- Use proper hygiene, and do not wear excessive amounts of perfume or cologne. Do not chew gum. Do not smoke near the premises before entering. Breath mints are appropriate and a good idea.
- Arrive around five minutes early. Plan ahead to make sure you know how long it will take to get to the location and find parking if necessary.
- Be prepared to wait if your host is running behind or is occupied with something critical for a period of time. Also be prepared for potential changes in your schedule or an unexpected ending of the shadow sooner than planned due to unforeseen circumstances that day for your host. Remember that your host's primary responsibility is to do her job.
- Be polite and respectful to receptionists and anyone who works for your host.
- Your shadow may include lunch. If so, your host will most likely offer to pay, but be prepared to buy your own lunch if a group goes together to a fast food establishment. Make sure you use good table manners at lunch and do not eat excessive amounts of food.
- Shake hands firmly with everyone you meet. Smile, look people in the eye, and thank them for this opportunity.

- Silence your cell phone, and do not text or use social media unless you are sitting in a waiting area while you wait for your host. Even if you are in a waiting area, do not watch videos, put in headphones, or play sounds on your phone out loud. While you are with others during your shadow day, the focus should be on them and the job experience. If your phone rings, let it go to voicemail. If you must check your phone, do so in the restroom, so that your hosts know you are completely focused on learning and getting the most out of their time.
- If you are not sure how to address someone, use Mr. or Ms., or Dr. if the person is clearly a medical doctor or if they use Dr. in their email signature or on their business card.
- It is okay to make some casual conversation and get to know your host, in addition to asking job-related questions. This can be helpful in making the day more enjoyable, but also emphasize listening more than talking.
- Don't be afraid to ask questions. Your host may be unsure of what to show you or tell you, so be prepared with questions.
- Expect to answer questions about yourself from people you encounter. They may ask where you are from, what you like to do, and why you are interested in their career field.
- Ask for business cards from people you meet so that you can begin to build your network of contacts in the field. If you meet someone during the day who expresses an interest in helping you, ask for that person's card and then connect with him or her later if appropriate. Make notes on the card as a reminder if necessary.
- Do not give out your personal phone number, email address, or social media connections to anyone if you are unclear about the reason for their request it and there is not a professional purpose for doing so, such as connecting you with additional job shadows or answering career questions. You can politely decline by asking if it would be okay to have their email address so you can follow up with them. If you have any concerns about further contact, you can ask your parents to send an email on your behalf or simply choose not to send anything.
- Thank everyone you meet for spending time with you and sharing information.

Internships and Part-time Jobs

Another way to try on a career is by doing a summer internship or taking a part-time job. Some employers in your community will take on a few high school students for internships in which they have an opportunity to work on a project and spend a lot of time doing both informational interviewing and job shadowing, but in a more informal manner. For high school students, these internship opportunities are most likely to be advertised directly through the school. Your teen should check with the school counseling office to see what may be available.

Part-time jobs may also be available in certain fields for high school students, although this depends greatly on how much education and expertise are required for that career. Sometimes there may be a part-time position that is clerical or running errands, but the point is that it gives your child an opportunity to be around those in a career field that interests them and get informal opportunities for informational interviewing and job shadowing. When considering such part-time jobs for the purpose of learning more about a career, it is important to make sure that the role will expose your teen to the types of individuals from whom he hopes to learn something and will not just be a source of cheap labor for menial tasks without any learning opportunities. A good way to determine this is to speak with students who previously worked at that organization or held that part-time job. Here again the school may have a longstanding relationship with local employers and may know which opportunities provided the best experiences for students in the past.

Online Communities

We have talked a lot about in-person experiences that can help students get a better sense of a career field, but there are also many online resources that can help add some perspective, and these are not the standard career profile sites that schools offer. It takes some Internet sleuthing to find the right resources, but we can recommend a few search terms that will help identify online resources that may provide more of an insider's look at specific career fields:

- "how to increase your earnings as a [career name]"
- "professional development for [career name]"
- "email newsletter for [job title]"

- "best blogs for [job title]"
- "why I am no longer a [job title]"
- "are there good jobs in [career field]"

Some of these search terms will lead to online articles that are more candid and expose some of the hot issues in the field, especially around job opportunities, how to get ahead, and compensation.

11

Is College Right for You?

There was a time when high schools took a more simplified view of how to prepare students for life after graduation. One group of students, sometimes small depending on the local economy, would be on a "college prep" track, taking the most academically challenging courses in English, history, science, foreign language, and math all four years. These students would go on to college and then perhaps study further to become doctors, lawyers, scientists, businesspeople, and other white-collar professionals. Another group of students, sometimes large in rural or industrial areas, would be on a vocational path, taking general foundation academic courses and then selecting a specific vocational track for technical learning, perhaps even finishing high school ready for a good entry-level skilled job in a well-paying blue-collar career path. It is a common misconception that these vocational tracks were seen as undesirable. In fact, depending on the town, spots for certain vocational training programs were highly competitive because of the local job opportunities at the time. Students would compete for the opportunity to get into technical courses for machinists, electricians, mechanics, or pipefitters.

Over the past three decades or so, this division between college-bound and career-track students has become more ambiguous and controversial. The cost of college has skyrocketed, growing wildly faster than average household earnings. Shaun distinctly remembers thumbing through a college guidebook around 1985 and seeing Stanford's annual tuition to be somewhere around $10,000 (it was in fact $10,476), which would be about $24,000, adjusting for inflation, in today's dollars. Compared to Stanford's current 2017 tuition of $45,195, that is an 88 percent increase in the real cost of tuition alone, much less other costs such as room and board, but we are not sure you would argue that students are getting close to 88 percent more economic or educational value from attending Stanford today than they would have from attending in 1985 if we adjust for inflation. Even if your child is well within the academic skill range to complete college course work and earn a degree, the question of whether there is a real return on this investment is not as clear as it would have been in 1985.

Everyone seems to know a story today of a college graduate with thousands of dollars in debt who is working in a service industry or blue-collar job that does not require a college degree. During the same period that college costs have skyrocketed, a vast range of good blue-collar industrial jobs have been sent overseas, lost to cheaper competition in developing countries, or eliminated through computers and automation. With the loss of these jobs came the loss of opportunity for many to take a high school diploma and build a career that supports a middle-class lifestyle with a good health care plan and a safe retirement, which has hollowed out many middle-class communities around the country. Yet we have also seen the emergence of an increasing number of what IBM is now calling "new-collar" jobs. At IBM, these are jobs like server technicians, database managers, and other information technology roles that fit somewhere between a technical trade and a professional career in terms of the level of education and expertise required. In some cases, employers are willing to fund the two-year associate degree or certification program that prepares a student for these jobs as part of on-the-job training.

How do you know if college will really be worth it? What does "return on investment" even mean when you are talking about a person's education, not just career preparation? And how do you know if college is a fit for your child, even if the economics make sense in abstract terms but he is not sure he can handle it or even wants it?

In this chapter we look at those questions and try to provide some helpful discussion topics for you and your son or daughter to sort through. In absolute dollars and percentage terms, college is one of the top two or three purchases people will make in their lifetime. It's worth spending some time seriously considering what college means to your teen, why she wants to go, and whether she has a realistic chance of getting what she expects out of it.

Why College?

First, let's spend some time addressing the question of whether college makes economic sense. It is completely true that college costs more in absolute terms today than it did thirty years ago, in some cases as much as 400 percent more, even after adjusting for inflation. We would assert that what colleges are delivering to students (the essential "product," if you will) has changed very little in terms of education, social development, civic engagement, and career preparation. Then why else would you be paying more? We believe the extra cost has come along with little meaningful long-term extra benefit to the student's life after college. The reasons for the extra cost are a complex mix of factors such as increased spending on administrative personnel, increased perks to compete for students (e.g., fancy new dorms, gyms), and the ability for colleges to charge more money when the federal government is happy to keep guaranteeing higher student loans that cover those increasing costs.

The United States offers more choices for students to attend college than any other country by far. Germany, a well-educated and economically competitive country, has about 60 percent fewer colleges, adjusted for population. Because we have so many more colleges in the United States, those colleges must compete more with each other to stay in business. Even though it sounds counterintuitive, raising its prices can actually make a college appear more prestigious and competitive in the marketplace. Few will admit it publicly, but a college is a business, and even if it is a nonprofit, that does not mean it can be a "negative profit." If there is a spending arms race to attract students, a college may face extinction if it refuses to participate unless it is one of the most prestigious institutions in the country.

All of this has little if anything to do with a direct improvement in instruction and student outcomes, the whole reason your teen would go to college in the first place. Professors' salaries have remained largely stagnant in real terms since the 1970s, and a much higher percentage of professors are part-time today than back then. Students are not coming out of college smarter, more employable, wiser, or happier than they did in 1970. And yet on average, college is still a good economic investment compared to not going to college at all. How can this be? Much of it has to do with how the employment landscape has changed and the Great Recession beginning in 2008 in particular. That recession accelerated a trend that was already happening, which is the reduction of low-skill, blue-collar, and clerical jobs due to automation; moving jobs to countries with cheaper labor; closing factories due to competition from emerging markets; and successful challenges to the power of organized labor in certain industries.

As we noted earlier in this book, the Georgetown University Center on Education and the Workforce published in a 2016 report that about 11.6 million new jobs had been created since the 2008 recession ended, and of those jobs, almost 99 percent went to people with some level of college education. Seventy-two percent of those jobs went to someone with at least a bachelor's degree. Only 80,000 jobs out of 11.6 million new jobs went to a person with nothing more than a high school diploma. According to the report, that trend has accelerated with each new recession over the last few decades. People holding a four-year degree (or higher) for the first time ever now make up a greater percentage of the workforce (36 percent) than students with only a high school diploma (34 percent). Office and administrative support, historically one of the largest segments of the working population, suffered a decline of 1.4 million positions during the last recession. There are still 1.6 million fewer construction positions than before the recession. While manufacturing jobs rebounded following the recession, more of these jobs than ever before require some kind of technical knowledge, and having at least an associate degree can provide a competitive advantage for applicants.

Large segments of our economy that used to rely on low-skill labor are finding ways to achieve more productivity with fewer people, and the smaller number of employees who remain are being asked to bring skills to the workplace that cannot be obtained solely in high school. Production industries employ only about 19 percent of today's workforce compared to 50 percent in 1947, whereas industries that rely on professional workers now employ 46 percent of today's workforce compared to 28 percent in 1947. The data are undeniable: college graduates across all degree types have lower unemployment rates than those without any college education.

What about earnings? According to a 2014 analysis of Labor Department statistics by the Economic Policy Institute in Washington, DC, the gap between what college graduates earn and what those without a degree earn has hit an all-time high. People in the United States with a college degree earned about 98 percent more an hour on average than people without a degree in 2013. That difference was only 64 percent in the early 1980s. So there is plenty of sound evidence that compared to people who don't have college degrees, college degree holders are likely to be more employed in the future, earn much higher wages on average, and hold jobs that provide important benefits such as health care coverage and retirement plans.

We are not implying that having a college degree is a guarantee of employment or a middle-class wage with solid benefits. A lot depends on your child's personal interests, aptitudes, circumstances, decisions, and work ethic. Some career fields pay much more on average than others, and some colleges provide a high-quality degree for a better price than others. Moreover, the economic landscape will never stop shifting, sometimes dramatically. College is an investment, and like any other investment opportunity, there are options that provide great returns for the price and options where you can get much less than you thought you would even when the cost is breathtaking and the marketing is slick. But the good news is that there are so many colleges in the United States that if students are thoughtful and spend an adequate amount of time exploring their options and understanding more about their potential career interests and earnings, there are many good choices that will greatly increase the likelihood that their life will be better off with a college degree than without one.

College has other benefits beyond the direct knowledge for employment in specific career fields. We would argue in many cases that some of the best career preparation from college comes from experiences outside the lecture hall. First, good colleges challenge students to develop critical thinking skills. Rather than just learning information and regurgitating it back in exams or papers, students need to learn to make their own inquiries into a question where the answer is not entirely clear and then develop arguments and defend them. The best colleges and program departments make students solve open-ended problems where the solutions may surprise even the professor. The professional jobs with the highest earnings potential and strongest employment stability will be roles that require us to solve the kinds of problems that computers and cheap offshore labor cannot. Colleges give students a toolbox of mental models and problem-solving strategies that they can apply to a wide range of problems regardless of the career field.[1,2,3,4]

Second, college provides opportunities to develop interpersonal and social/emotional skills that can enrich students' lives and improve their career prospects. Many college courses require students to work in teams and deal with the challenges of coordinating group action, leading others, and coping with uncomfortable situations like a slacking teammate. Students who take seminar-style courses will learn to express and defend their ideas in front of a group and deal with public critique. Almost every college offers semester-long public speaking courses that require students to present in front of large groups. And in order to succeed, almost all college students at one point or another will need to advocate for themselves and ask for help from a variety of professors, teaching assistants, or peers.

College often exposes students to a diversity of ideas, religions, eth-nicities, and regional and international cultures. This exposure can help them learn to respect ideas and backgrounds very different from their own, which increases their ability to relate, lead, and problem-solve with people from many different places. These are among the soft skills that distinguish high-potential employees in a workplace and put them in a position to become leaders who work on high-profile initiatives such as international expansion, cross-functional innovation teams, and special task forces. Even in highly sophisticated technical fields, someone has to translate ideas back and forth between technical and nontechnical staff, and someone has to help make a group of highly educated geniuses function as a successful team. Many of the best colleges deliberately ensure that students are working as much toward this type of knowledge as their more formal subject matter expertise because they want to produce successful alumni who will reflect well on the college and give back to their alma mater.

A third benefit of college is a chance to establish a social network that can provide a foundation for both lifelong friendship and career networking opportunities. In a well-known TED talk, Robert Waldinger, a clinical professor of psychiatry at Harvard Medical School, pointed out one of the primary findings from a seventy-five-year-long clinical study on human health and happiness. "Over and over in these 75 years," he pronounced, "our study has shown that the people who fared the best were the people who leaned into relationships with family, with friends, and with community." Few places and times in life provide as much opportunity to forge lasting friendships as college does. Many people meet lifelong friends there because they have extended periods of time where they are around others in a variety of settings, bump into interesting new people unexpectedly, and have a chance to meet repeatedly and really get to know someone well.

Finally, a fourth benefit of college is something your child might not yet appreciate, which is the potential exposure to completely new career options. Students frequently change their major. Both of us certainly did, and they were very big changes. Even with all of the thought that your child is putting into such a big decision as college and career, it is presumptuous to assume that eighteen-year-olds truly know everything about themselves until they get to interact more with the real world and get exposed to new ideas. Most colleges offer a wide range of majors. Larger universities in particular provide a vast array of course subjects and potential career connections. By attending college, your child may discover interesting and lucrative career options that never would have occurred to her until she was exposed to them through a chance encounter with another student or a professor.

All of this may sound wonderful, but what if your child will be the first in your family to go to college and will be having these new experiences alone, away from home, without being able to ask you about your own experiences from college when he encounters the inevitable stumble or hiccup? You and your child both may be worried he will fail or get homesick and possibly be embarrassed. Or you may worry that he will feel out of place because most other students on campus are not like him and do not share a common background and cultural experience. Perhaps you wonder if your child can handle that or if you should encourage him to walk into that situation. This is a legitimate concern and something you should discuss with your child openly.

If yours is a lower-income family or one with an ethnic/cultural background that is not very typical at your teen's chosen college, she may face challenges that many other students at that college do not worry about. It can be isolating, overwhelming, and frustrating, especially if your child feels extra pressure to succeed as the first in the family to go to college. But it can also help your child develop self-confidence by proving to herself that she can stick to something important even when it gets challenging or unpleasant. The most effective way for people to build self-confidence is by taking on an increasingly difficult set of challenges and overcoming them.

Many colleges are trying very hard to find high-potential students from more diverse backgrounds, and most provide extra support and advice to those students. Your child will not be completely alone in facing those challenges and can turn to adults at the college for help when needed. In addition, some research studies have shown that students with a demonstrated ability to complete four-year college-level work (from their grade point average or state test scores) will be more likely to finish college and earn a degree if they attend the more challenging four-year college rather than the less challenging two-year college that may be close to home. This may sound counterintuitive, but researchers believe it is due to the effect of increased expectations of professors and peers at a four-year college. Just by being there, everyone around them will assume they are capable of succeeding. Your child may rise to that expectation rather than fall short. Ultimately this will depend on your child's unique goals, strengths, and personality, but we encourage you to have the confidence that if your child has the ability to handle the academic work, is willing to work hard, and will ask for help, she can likely earn a four-year degree and transform her life in the process. And if you still have doubts, don't hesitate to ask the college how it could provide extra support to her in overcoming these obstacles, especially if she has already received an acceptance letter and financial aid offer.

We have discussed the economic and personal benefits of going to college, but we would be naive to state that there is no risk or downside potential in attending college, especially if costs are problematic. As we have discussed in detail, college now costs in real terms far more than it did thirty years ago, and those cost increases do not seem to be slowing down or resulting in any noticeable increase in the quality of the product. Some education analysts and entrepreneurs believe this increasing cost is like the housing bubble prior to the recession of 2008 and that higher education is on the cusp of a massive change in how it is delivered and how much it costs. While it does seem that the cost increases cannot be sustained indefinitely, we believe that the majority of colleges will stick around with a familiar model of doing things, and prices will remain relatively high as long as the best jobs require a college education.

Like any business, some colleges offer a great value for the price and some offer much less value for the same price. There is such a thing as a "good deal" in college education. If you were on a quixotic mission to deliberately find a bad deal, the two places you would look first are private for-profit colleges by far and then, to a lesser extent, private nonprofit colleges. Some of these colleges are quite good and work hard to provide a world-class education, and do their best to offer as much financial assistance as possible to students with need. But some of these colleges are very expensive and do not have a track record of providing greater benefits for that cost than your child could get from a cheaper public college or university. Unfortunately, it will require some good sleuthing on your part to distinguish which colleges or programs are the real deal and which ones are overpriced. Here are some things to consider:

- *Graduation rate.* Find out what percentage of students earn a degree. According to the U.S. Department of Education, fewer than 60 percent of first-time, full-time undergraduate students earn a bachelor's degree within six years, however this figure varies dramatically among colleges. Compare this number for each college your teenager is considering, and don't be afraid to ask a college why its number is so low or what advising programs it has in place to ensure that students stay on track and get help when they need it.
- *Employment statistics and earnings.* Look for statistics on employment and earnings after graduation. This should include the percentage of graduates who find a job within a year after graduation and any information on average earnings. If your child is considering a private for-profit college (e.g., a nursing school, an IT tech program), you should absolutely be able to get this information from the school; if you do not, cross it off the list. Some private for-profits are notorious for promising gainful employment and then failing to deliver. Over 90 percent of their funding comes from student loans guaranteed by the federal government, so if their students fail to get jobs and cannot pay off their loans, it is no problem for them because Uncle Sam picks up the tab. You should also look at average salaries for the career field your child intends to pursue and have a candid discussion about what he wants to achieve in life in terms of both professional accomplishment and financial means. One of the most common ways that a college education can become a burden instead of a benefit is when there is a large disparity between the cost of that education and the potential earnings from the degree pathway that your child has chosen. If your child is passionate about being a kindergarten teacher in a poor urban community but will graduate with over $80,000 in student loan debt, this is not going to go well for her financially and may delay her ability to obtain a mortgage, get married, or live on her own for years after graduation. Maybe there are other intangible benefits

to attending that college that left your child with $80,000 in debt, like living in a lively New York City neighborhood or studying Shakespeare in England for a semester. That may be worth it for some people, but either way, we strongly encourage you to discuss with your child the concept of trying to align the cost of her college education with the long-term value she is likely to realize as a result.

- *Average debt.* Try to find the average student debt of a graduate. This can help you get a sense of how well the college is working to help students meet their financial needs. Some colleges offer financial aid packages that consist of a small grant or tuition discount ("merit aid") and then an opportunity to fund the bulk of their expensive tuition with student loans and a campus job. This is not much of a financial aid package, and money that someday must come back out of your child's pocket is not "assistance."

- *Average class size.* One potential sign of a college that may be providing lower value for the price is average class size, especially if it is a smaller private college. Class size at large public colleges will sometimes be inflated due to big lecture hall–style courses that meet freshman require-ments, but this would be unusual at a smaller private college. It's helpful to compare these numbers with other well-known reputable colleges even if your child will not apply just to get a sense of whether the numbers seem off-base.

- *Alumni.* Try to speak with graduates to learn more about their experience and, in particular, whether they found the kind of career success they had hoped for from their degree. If your child is hoping to pursue a very specific career field, see if the college will put her in touch with recent graduates from that program.

- *Special assistance.* Perhaps a college has reached out to your child because of his diverse ethnic or socioeconomic background and has told your child that it is "looking for students like you." Some colleges truly work hard to create a welcoming place for diverse students, but others may tell a good story without backing it up with meaningful services and programs. Ask the college what kind of support it offers, if any, for students who may be from atypical backgrounds. Also, many colleges offer specialized support services for students with learning differences. Students with significant learning differences have a higher risk of not graduating and leaving college early with student debt to pay off. You can search online for colleges that have the best programs for these students, and you can ask the admissions office for information as well.

- *Books and online lists.* A lot of college counselors and authors over the years have done some research on colleges that offer a great education and interesting experiences, often for a reasonable price because they are not the biggest names out there. A couple that we recommend exploring are *Colleges That Change Lives: 40 Schools That Will Change the Way You Think about Colleges* by Loren Pope, *Where You Go Is Not Who You'll Be: An Antidote to the College Admissions Mania* by Frank Bruni, and *The Hidden Ivies, 3rd Edition: 63 of America's Top Liberal Arts Colleges and Universities* by Howard Greene and Matthew W. Greene. You can also find several good online resources recommending good-value colleges if you do a search for "best-value colleges."

If you do the kind of research we recommend, it's likely that your teen will end up at a quality college with a good price, or at least the best price relative to quality that you can find, even if the cost is still a stretch for your family. This still does not guarantee, though, that the college is right for your teen. You also need to help her take a good look inward and explore her attitudes and aptitudes to make sure it is the right choice for her personally. Here are some things to consider:

- *Attitude toward school.* Does your teen enjoy school or at least see it as a necessary and natural step in achieving goals? Or does she look at school as a constant battle to overcome boredom and pointless frustration? As we have mentioned elsewhere, many students take longer than four years to earn a bachelor's degree. If your child feels that she was pressured to attend college and is constantly battling her own indifference toward school work, there is a good chance she could end up drifting aimlessly, wasting both time and money, and possibly not even earning a degree while getting stuck with burdensome debt. The employment prospects and the value of a degree for a student who wanders through college are not going to be nearly as good as they could have been.
- *Aptitude for school.* College-level course work is generally harder than most high school work. It requires a more intense pace of reading, writing, and studying. And there will be much less formal structure to guide students as they work. Students are on their own to make sure they are keeping up. They need to make choices about how to spend their time that high school students don't have to make. Does your child have self-discipline, time management skills, and solid study skills? If he has learning differences, has he spent time to learn about special programs and accommodations that a specific college may offer?
- *Self-determination.* Ultimately the students who get the most out of college are the ones who are goal oriented and proactive about pursuing their

career ambitions. They know why they are in college, what they expect to get out of it, and how it relates to their long-term plan in life. They have thought about how much college costs and how much they intend to earn. Most important, they are not wandering aimlessly, hoping that college will somehow lead to good things one day. Does your teen have a strong sense of self-determination and a belief that she can control her destiny and make choices about her future rather than waiting for something to happen to her? College is too expensive to be a passive experience.

In some cases, your child may aspire to a career field that typically requires a college degree but she did not have the academic strengths or other attributes to qualify for a good financial aid package to attend a four-year college. Or maybe your child needs a four-year degree for a certain career, but you are uncertain about whether she has the temperament or academic skills to make it through just yet. There are a couple of options to consider. First, there is community college, and we have dedicated chapter 14 to this topic in which we discuss how community college can be part of a four-year degree plan and some of the potential pitfalls as well. Second, an increasing number of employers are providing specialized training or funding an associate degree in certain fields for their employees. You can search the web for more information about these opportunities with terms like "new-collar jobs" or "gray-collar jobs." These career fields can be a good way for someone to gain some work experience and firm up career interests while still offering long-term career pathways to workers who go back to college and earn a degree and then return to the field in a more advanced capacity such as a manager or subject matter expert. Another option to consider is a gap year, in which your child takes a year off between high school and college. This can provide time for her to experience life outside of a classroom, possibly working or exploring a career field through an internship. This break from school can provide more time to help her decide if she is really committed to additional education or to develop more emotional maturity and focus before investing in an expensive college degree.

An Important Warning

We hear stories all the time about students who decide to go back to college and pursue a four-year degree after going to community college, earning a certificate, studying at a vocational training program, or getting some partial college credit from a previous attempt at a degree. Often this is because they have found their career choices to be too limited, or they are not earning what they had hoped within a trade or profession. In many cases, these students are devastated to learn that some or all of the credit they earned in their previous education will not be recognized as valid credit toward a four-year degree at the new college they are attending. If your child thinks that a four-year degree might be in the future but wants to try something else first, it is worth spending time to research whether any of the credits he earns now will be transferable to a four-year-degree program later. He may accumulate debt from pursuing these initial studies and then find that he cannot afford to take on the additional debt to complete a four-year degree later because so few credits transfer. Some thoughtful planning and research ahead of time could either help your child avoid this issue or at least go in fully aware of a potential roadblock to switching back to the pursuit of a four-year degree later in life.

All things considered, if your child attends a reasonably good college, pays a reasonably good price, and gets reasonably good grades, it is hard to argue with the likelihood that she will be enriched financially, intellectually, and socially. The key, as with so many other things, is doing the homework. It's important to take the time to research and compare colleges based on how successful their graduates are relative to the price. It's also important that you and your child have an open and honest conversation about her appetite and aptitude for school.

12 | Can You Afford College?

College is expensive. According to the College Board, one year of tuition and fees at a private college averaged just under $33,500 in 2016. That's more than 50 percent of the average income earned by a U.S. household. Paying for college is an investment in the future, but the cost can also be one of the biggest stressors for families. Luckily, there are ways to help pay for college, but it takes time and work to identify them. The first step is figuring out the true cost of attendance. From there you can assess your personal resources and investigate financial aid, scholarships, loans, and other ways to pay for college.

What's the Real Price of College?

Every college publishes a "sticker price," which reflects the annual cost of tuition and fees. The sticker price can vary dramatically from the actual cost of attendance, however. Factors such as additional fees can add to the cost of college, while scholarships and grants may reduce it. The true cost of college doesn't have to be a mystery, and there are ways to get a peek at what you'd actually have to pay. To begin, it helps to understand the terminology as well as the tools that are available to help predict the true price of college.

Tuition, Fees, and Other Costs

Colleges publish the cost of tuition and fees on their websites, and this information can also be found in college search engines and college ranking magazines. Tuition, which pays for instruction and the operating costs of an institution, varies from college to college and can be as low as $4,000 per year to as high as $55,000 per year. Fees, which support additional campus services such as information technology, health services, and parking, are incremental to the tuition cost. If your child is staying on campus, you can also expect to pay additional costs for room and board.

Expected Family Contribution

The approximate amount of the tuition, fees, and other costs that you'll need to cover out-of-pocket is known as the Expected Family Contribution (EFC). Using various inputs, your EFC weighs parental income, assets, number of children in the household, and other factors. You can find EFC calculators on many websites, and calculating your EFC is an important first step in the financial aid process. An EFC calculation is a rough estimate, however, since it relies on limited data and doesn't evaluate extenuating circumstances. As your child's college search process progresses, you'll be able to develop more precise estimates using other tools.

Net Price Calculator

When your child begins to narrow the list of possibilities, you'll want to look at each college's net price calculator. The calculator is an institution-specific way to forecast the amount you'll pay after projected grants and scholarships have been awarded. Because more scholarships are typically awarded by private colleges and universities than public ones, the calculator is most helpful for these institutions. The calculator can typically be found on each institution's financial aid website.

FAFSA4caster

The FAFSA4caster is another tool to make projections in the process of paying for college. The 4caster allows families to complete a mock FAFSA (Free Application for Federal Student Aid, described in more detail later this in chapter) using financial and personal information to make an estimate of federal financial aid eligibility. You and your teen can also use the data to estimate costs for specific colleges factoring in this FAFSA information.

True Costs

EFC and Net Price Calculators, the FAFSA4caster, and other ways to estimate college costs are helpful, but you really won't know the true cost of each college until after your child has been accepted to the institution and has received a financial aid award letter. Based on that letter, and the details of any financial aid award you may receive, you're in a better position to address the question of whether you can afford college.

Can You Afford College?

Regardless of family income, nearly every parent is bound to ask: Can we afford college? There are ways to pay for college, but navigating the process requires careful thought and planning. Loans, grants, and other means help to construct a plan to pay the bills before, after, and during college.

Ways to Pay for College

Grants

Grants are money awarded to families who show financial need as determined by the FAFSA. They do not need to be paid back and are generally awarded on a yearly basis. Federal grants, specifically the Pell Grant, are the most common grants available for college students. A Pell Grant normally does not cover all of the tuition and fees that students need to pay for college, so they are typically supplemented with other forms of aid.

Loans

Student loans come in many forms, and unlike grants, they need to be repaid. The most common types are Direct Subsidized Loans, Direct Unsubsidized Loans, and Direct PLUS loans, all of which are part of the U.S. federal government's William D. Ford Federal Direct Loan Program. Private student loans are also available.

Direct Subsidized Loans are available to undergraduate students who qualify based on financial need. These loans don't accrue interest until after the student has graduated (or left) college.

Direct Unsubsidized Loans are available to undergraduate, graduate, and professional students regardless of family income. Unlike subsidized loans, these loans begin to accrue interest as soon as they are dispersed.

Students can receive a combination of subsidized and unsubsidized loans, but there is a cap on the amount that they receive. These loans typically do not require repayment until after graduation or the student leaves college.

Direct PLUS Loans are available to parents of dependent undergraduate students or to graduate or professional students and can help to pay additional education expenses that aren't covered by financial aid.

Students and families may also be able to borrow additional funds for college through private student loans from banks, credit unions, and other lenders. These loans typically carry higher interest rates than federal loans, but unlike federal loans they can be used to pay other college expenses beyond tuition and fees.

Scholarships

Scholarships come in many forms. Scholarships are funds that do not need to be repaid that students can use for college expenses. For many students, scholarships can be an important resource when it comes to affording college. Often, the biggest scholarships that a student receives are institutional scholarships awarded directly by the college he or she is attending. Institutional scholarships are more common for private colleges and universities than public institutions. It is always a good idea to inquire at the admissions office about types of scholarships available because they may require special applications, auditions, or essays.

Outside scholarships are another way students can earn money to defray the cost of college. These scholarships can come in many forms and with different requirements. They can be offered by anyone, from large corporations to small town community organizations. Some teens treat the scholarship search and application process like a job, and a lot of times their work will pay off. Students should check with their schools on the latest scholarships available, and parents should check with their places of work and worship for availability.

529 Plans

Parents who start saving early can help their teens as they enter college. A 529 or other savings plan can be started as early as birth and are run by individual states. These plans can come in two main forms, a savings plan or a prepaid tuition plan, and they can be used at eligible colleges nationwide. Some setup is required, so checking with a 529 administrator or financial planner can help ensure proper planning and allocation for this program.

Is the ROI Worth It?

The term *return on investment* (ROI) is widely used in the financial world. But the concept is increasingly used when evaluating college options. Instead of asking, "Can I afford college?" many families and potential college students are being more thoughtful about the potential return on investment from a college education—considering both the time and costs required. Although it can sound transactional, it is a good idea to ask a college what your ROI may be. When evaluating ROI for a particular college or program, consider the net cost of college (including tuition, fees, and expenses less grants and scholarships), graduation rate, time to graduation, typical loan amount, and employment prospects after graduation. Calculators and rankings exist for ROI, but this number is extremely personal and must take into account each teen's unique situation.

Applying for Financial Aid

According to the National Center for Education Statistics, more than 80 percent of first-time, full-time college students are eligible for financial aid, but many families choose not to apply for it because they assume they aren't eligible. As a result, some of these families may decide college isn't affordable or may pay thousands of dollars more than they would otherwise. The best way to know what you're eligible to receive is to apply for aid every year.

What Is the FAFSA?

The FAFSA is the federal form that postsecondary institutions use to evaluate the amount of grants, loans, and sometimes even scholarships for which students are eligible. It uses family tax information throughout its online form, which can then be sent to individual institutions for an evaluation of student aid.

It's a common misconception that completing the FAFSA is a waste of time for anyone making more than $50,000. *Every* college student should complete the FAFSA *every* year because it opens the door to scholarship and low-cost loan opportunities. When the FAFSA is sent to a college and matched with an application, the college formulates an award letter. This letter lists the amount of grants, loans, and merit aid that an applicant may receive for that school year.

Another myth of the FAFSA is that the process is too hard. It used to be the case that you had to file (or at least complete) your taxes from the current filing year prior to filing the FAFSA, and even then you had to complete page after page of information. But now the tax information on the FAFSA can be taken from taxes you filed for the previous year and the FAFSA website is easier to navigate than ever before. In fact, the FAFSA has implemented the IRS Retrieval Tool that pulls filed tax returns to autocomplete much of the FAFSA form. The FAFSA website (http://fafsa.ed.gov) has all of the information to walk you through the process of completing the FAFSA. Keep in mind that the FAFSA is a *free* tool, so you should never be charged to complete or file your forms.

CSS PROFILE

Almost four hundred colleges use an additional form known as the CSS PROFILE to determine eligibility for nonfederal student aid. The PROFILE is similar to the FAFSA but collects more information, including extenuating circumstances that may help your teen qualify for additional funding. Unlike the FAFSA, the College Board charges a processing fee each time you submit a PROFILE form to a college. But like the FAFSA, the PROFILE is well worth the time and effort—and in this case the fee—because it may lead to aid that assists in making college a bit less costly.

Keep in mind that financial aid offers have to be accepted before any money is dispersed. Read the instructions from each institution carefully, and if you have questions, ask your school counselor or the college's financial aid office for assistance. At some point, everyone goes through this process for the first time, and financial aid offices are prepared for this. They can explain each aspect of the award letter to you and discuss the pros and cons of the award.

Build Your Dream Team

Figuring out how to pay for college isn't solely on the shoulders of parents. By starting early and building a team of advocates and experts, you can demystify the process. It is easy to feel overwhelmed when faced with the daunting task of going along this path; creating a financial aid dream team makes the journey much easier.

The dream team of the financial aid process can work hand in hand to make the financial aid process much less stressful. The key to success in the financial aid process is involving stakeholders early in the game and asking questions up front and often.

So who is on this dream team, and how do you even begin the conversation? Although it might differ school by school and college by college, there are some main players who are trained to help you through the process.

School Counselor

School counselors are employed in all states and in just about every high school in the country. Licensed school counselors are trained not only to help kids with emotional and academic questions, but with the college planning process as well. The school counselor is empowered to be a student advocate, a shoulder to lean on, and a source of extensive knowledge about the college admissions and financial aid process. Often school counselors hold financial aid awareness nights and workshops to walk parents of juniors and seniors through the financial aid application process.

College Admissions Counselor

One of the first faces that a prospective student associates with a college is the admissions counselor. The admissions counselor is the first point of contact when it comes to initial questions about financial aid. These counselors are equipped to let you and your teen know the types of scholarships available, what the average merit aid is, and the specifics about tuition, fees, and other estimated expenses. College admissions counselors also tend to know a lot about the FAFSA, so they are a resource in the application process as well. College admissions counselors are there to help, not to be a roadblock to admissions and financial aid.

Financial Aid Office

Every college financial aid office works hand in hand with the admissions office to ensure that applicants have the best and most timely information needed. In turn, teens should feel that they can contact the financial aid office for questions they have. Especially after filing the FAFSA or receiving the award letter, families should lean on the experts in their specific college's financial aid office to clarify any questions they may have throughout the process.

Your Child

Believe it or not, your child can be part of her own financial aid process. Yes, it might be easiest to call on members of the dream team yourself, but the more she is involved in the conversation about financial aid, the more she will feel that she has a stake in the game. Juniors and seniors who are involved early learn communication skills, the financial aid process, and how to advocate for themselves. Kids should know what they are signing and when, and they should be involved in their own loan counseling requirements.

Other Ways to Pay for College

Loans, grants, and scholarships aren't the only way to pay for college. There are some not-so-common ways many people use to supplement the cost of college. Kids can get creative to bank some credits, earn money, and save some money to pay for expenses.

Dual Enrollment

High school students all over the country choose to take dual-enrollment courses to earn credits for college. From a couple of credits through a college in the school's program to a full two years by dual enrollment at a local college, dual-enrollment programs provide a vehicle for teens to get a taste of college-level course work all while saving money through earning credit as a high school student. Credits from dual-enrollment programs transfer to many colleges, but not all of them. Check with colleges you're considering before committing to an intensive dual-enrollment program.

Testing Out

Some options allow teens to show that they can do college-level work through taking tests. Some of these tests occur while the teen is still in high school and some just prior to coming to campus for their freshman year of college. Although these tests might not be a one-to-one match with classes, they may help students to avoid zero-credit courses or enroll in the next most rigorous course in their college major.

Advanced Placement (AP) and International Baccalaureate (IB) tests are one way that high school students can get a jump start on college credit. To earn college credit, students must take the correlating course in high school and then pass the exam at the end of the school year. Not all colleges offer credit for AP or IB courses, and when they do, it's at varying degrees. College admissions counselors can assist with this topic throughout the admissions process.

Colleges may also offer students the chance to earn credits or to skip introductory courses through various exams. Placement exams are designed to ensure that new students are in the correct course and that they are ready to take college-level classes. Those who do not score high enough on these exams are sometimes placed in remedial or zero-credit courses, which add to tuition fees.

CLEP allows students to take exams that many colleges recognize for college credit. As with AP and IB exams, not all colleges accept CLEP for credit or in the place of required courses. It is always recommended to check with the college prior to taking these exams.

Military

The military presents a variety of options when it comes to postsecondary opportunities. Typically people imagine joining the military as going off to boot camp and immediately beginning active duty. This route can help students pay for college (with the GI Bill), but if the initial goal is to attend college directly after high school, there are ways to be active in the military and be on campus at the same time.

One of the most intense postsecondary military experiences is to go to a military academy. Here, there is no tuition for students. Military academies are typically extremely competitive and require service after graduation. A more common path that students take during college is through a Reserve Officers' Training Corps (ROTC) program. ROTC allows students to attend a traditional college or university while being involved in ROTC programming outside classes. ROTC students typically receive full tuition with expenses paid, and there is a military enlistment requirement following college graduation.

A Balancing Act

If you commit to paying for college, there are ways to do it. For most families, there will be some give-and-take and sacrifices that need to be made. There are questions that parents should ask themselves and their children, as well as questions that should be asked of colleges. By going through this checklist and responding honestly, you can truly answer the question "Can I afford college?"

- *"Are we willing to take out loans?"* Do you want only student loans, or are parents willing to take loans as well? Are you willing to take unsubsidized loans? Can you be flexible in your child's college choice? A big discussion in college fit is whether the college is affordable. Don't discount colleges that may have high sticker prices but provide a lot of merit- or need-based aid.
- *"What's the backup plan?"* Sometimes the ROI for a college is just too low. What is the backup plan for this? Is starting at a community college an option? Does it help to take dual-enrollment credits or to add to the list?
- *"What's the plan?"* Is there a set price that parents will pay toward college out of pocket? Will a summer job be required? Who pays for books and other expenses? Who will be paying back the loans?

These questions along with some self-reflection will help you to create a plan to pay for college. Students should be involved every step of the way so they can remain informed and begin to develop lifelong financial decision-making skills. Paying for college is not always easy, but it can be done.

13

Does It Matter Where You Go to College?

Most kids develop an awareness of college at an early age. Maybe they begin to cheer for the local college baseball team or maybe a parent is passionate about her alma mater.

As they progress through their late elementary and middle school experience, kids become more familiar with the purpose of college. They begin to connect college to career and understand the effect their school work has on their college applications. The conversation turns serious as they enter their first couple of years of high school. The pool of colleges can feel overwhelming, and many kids don't know where to start their search.

As they approach high school graduation, the conversation turns to college fit. Instead of looking at the college rankings and pulling out the top ten institutions to apply to, teens are becoming purposeful in their college search. One college does not fit all, and it's up to kids, parents, schools, and institutions to help them match academically, personally, and socially to the right college. The more (and earlier) that kids investigate fit, the more likely they are to be successful in college.

What Is Fit?

College fit is more than choosing a college based on prestige, proximity, or parent legacy. For kids, college fit is a combination of factors that allows them to be set up for success. And sometimes what fits may not be exactly what kids (or their parents) expect it to be. There are many determinants of college fit, and what constitutes fit for one student may be completely different for another. Kids should ask themselves certain questions when they consider college fit to develop a deliberate and thoughtful list of colleges to consider, apply to, and eventually attend.

Questions to Determine Fit

Will This College Help Me Meet My Career Goals?

This question goes beyond majors offered at a college. High school students should explore college majors and ensure the colleges they are interested in offer programs in their interest areas, especially if a major must be declared on enrollment. However, many colleges offer career-oriented programs that complement traditional, classroom-based learning. Some institutions provide the ability to job shadow, intern, or observe professionals in students' careers of interest. For example, many education programs require their students to sit in on an elementary classroom for a certain period of time to fulfill the requirements of introductory education classes. This allows them to decide if they actually like the intensity of a classroom. Colleges that provide experiential or hands-on learning do their students a favor by allowing them to preview a career before they get too deep into their college major.

Another way colleges may support students in their career planning is by helping them develop a strong professional network where they might find internship or job shadowing opportunities. Some colleges have a long history of incorporating alumni into their career services program, hosting networking sessions, mentoring opportunities, and even scholarships. Colleges that don't have strong alumni associations can still provide excellent connections to career and internship opportunities through relevant community connections.

Spending time on campus is another way for high school juniors and seniors to determine whether a college can help them meet their career goals. In preparation for a campus visit, encourage kids to schedule appointments with the admissions staff, career center, and the academic department heads of the majors they are interested in. These meetings can help them get answers to specific career questions, including these:

- Are there any opportunities to explore careers related to my major within my first two years of college?
- What is your job placement rate?
- What are some examples of jobs people in my major have taken upon graduation?
- Does the career center offer career preparation classes or events? How early can I attend these?
- What connections do alumni have to the college? Do they offer internships or networking opportunities?

Will I Be Successful at This College?

"Success" at college can take on a number of meanings. More and more, graduation rates, specifically six-year graduation rates, have become a major component of the college search. All colleges measure and publish their graduation rates, and this information should be at the forefront of the college fit conversation. A poor graduation rate can mean a lot of things, so it's good to gather more information about the number. For example, at community colleges many students enter with the intention of taking one or two classes to bolster a specific skill. Since these students don't complete a degree program, they can negatively affect graduation rate even though they achieved their personal goals. Ask colleges about the factors affecting their graduation rate, including why they think students are not graduating from their institution. Perhaps more important, ask what supports they have in place to ensure their students persist and succeed through graduation.

Another way teens can assess their potential success at an institution is to ask questions related to academic success. This is where fit truly comes into play.

Some kids thrive in a large-group setting, attending lecture courses and taking tests to assess their content knowledge. Anonymity is fine with them when it comes to the classroom, and they prefer to study for tests and write papers instead of actively engaging in classroom conversations.

Others may prefer a small classroom setting. By being in a classroom where professors take attendance and involve them in active conversation, students can soak in the content knowledge and are measured not solely by multiple-choice assessments but through group projects, classroom participation, and presentations to their classmates.

Neither of these situations is better than the other, but when teens recognize how and where they thrive, they can seriously begin to consider how they personally will fit at the institution.

Another factor related to academic success is rigor. Colleges want to see applicants' grades, course rigor, and test scores to see if they match the rigor of their own academic programs. Institutions vary with the rigor they demand in their classes, and the fact that an applicant is admitted to a "reach school" doesn't necessarily mean he'll find success in the classroom. In fact, this may be completely the opposite. No one should attend an extremely academically challenging institution without being able to match that level of rigor. This is a hard conversation to have with teens, but having this discussion up front will help them realize that success in college is a personal endeavor that goes far beyond just "getting in" to a competitive school.

Other questions to ask colleges to determine fit include these:

- What is the average class size?
- Are first- and second-year classes typically lectures or seminars? Is there an opportunity for discussion in class?
- What services are in place to support students?
- Is an academic advisor assigned to every student? How often do they check in with students?
- Are professors required to have office hours or study groups?
- Is there a tutoring center on campus?
- How do my GPA and test scores compare to the average of students who are admitted?
- What is the average academic profile (e.g., number of AP courses, advanced courses, dual credit) of admitted students?

Do I Feel Comfortable on Campus?

Although success is often thought of in terms of surviving academically while in college, campus life often contributes to the retention (or lack thereof) of students. During campus visits, student tour guides talk a lot about dining on campus, cocurriculars, dorm life, and volunteer opportunities. This information shouldn't be dismissed as just a way to sell the college. Students spend only about fifteen to twenty hours each week in the college classroom. If they live on campus, the rest of the time will be spent eating in the dining hall, playing sports, spending time with friends, and interacting with people in the community (along with studying . . . hopefully).

Questions teens should ask during a campus tour or of students or college representatives include:

- Do you feel safe walking on campus? Have there been any recent crimes?
- Is there somewhere I can go if I am feeling lonely or sad?
- What activities exist that match my interests and strengths?
- Can I try lunch in the dining center while I'm visiting?

Can I Afford to Attend This College?

As we explored in depth in chapter 12, it's important to consider affordability as an integral part of college fit. Taking on an unmanageable level of debt or having to leave college because of the cost is not beneficial to students, parents, or the institution. College affordability isn't just related to the amount of scholarships and grants received. It means graduating with a reasonable amount of loans and then being able to pay off loans by obtaining gainful employment after graduation.

College affordability is a personal question, but teens and families should seriously consider the return on investment when investigating potential colleges. This conversation should also be had at the beginning of the college search process. A "dream" school should be a dream school only if it's affordable.

Some colleges get creative in helping to make attendance affordable for their students, so questions should always be asked through the discovery process—for example:

- What is the price I'll have to pay out of pocket?
- How much money will I have to borrow through loans?
- What other costs are associated with attending this institution (e.g., housing, books, fees, food)?
- Are there additional scholarships or methods of funding that are available to me to help afford attending?
- What are the most common jobs for those who graduate with my major, and what is the average salary?

Building a Smart College Application List

We encourage kids to start thinking about college at an early age and to start keeping a list of where they may want to attend. But the purpose of this list will change over time.

In elementary school, the opportunities are endless. College awareness is commonly related to sports or alumni connections, and kids recognize colleges in various parts of the country (or world) and begin to attach to them. Sometimes it sticks, but most times it doesn't. In middle school, the concept of career and the actual meaning of college become clearer. Kids also begin to have opinions on whether they'd like to go far away from home—or near the ocean, in the mountains—or attend while they're still living with their parents or grandparents.

In high school that college list takes on a whole new meaning. When reality sets in, kids begin to build their list more purposefully. In early high school, the list might be based on where friends are going, where their parents have attended, or their favorite sports teams, but it also starts to be influenced by college majors of interest. During the junior and senior years, it gets real. College visits begin, college admissions counselors start making contact, and their mailbox and inbox begin to fill up.

Building a purposeful college application list takes more than reading picture-perfect pamphlets. A college list starts out broad and then narrows to level of fit. In the summer before junior year, teens should get serious about college and discuss in a low-pressure way with friends, school staff, and family members to prepare for what's ahead.

Building a smart college list means more than applying to all of the most selective schools. In fact, applying to a large number of colleges can be more harmful than beneficial to kids, making the college admissions process more of a contest and less about finding the right fit—and consuming a considerable amount of time that is better spent on high school coursework and activities. Effective college admissions planning should be based on a series of strategic decisions, not a game of darts.

So how can kids construct a purposeful list that provides the best fit? It starts with throwing out all the predispositions to the college search. Instead of looking at college rankings, selectivity, who is making the NCAA championships, or where their friends are going, teens need to make the college search about *them*.

The first step to building a purposeful list is to figure out what is the most important part of fit. Maybe a teen fits in best in a large city or a rural location where everyone knows her name. Maybe the most important thing is to live close to home or to branch out and go to a different state. Perhaps affordability or academic fit will be the most important.

Start Broad

Teens often start the college search with what they know and stay within their comfort zone of familiar institutions. With more than 4,000 two- and four-year colleges in the United States alone, it's worth going in with an open mind. Encourage your teen to explore all the possibilities; he may be pleasantly surprised. Online college search tools can help kids discover colleges that fit their needs but are not familiar institutions. Challenge them to add three colleges that fit them but that they may never have considered to their first list of colleges. They may be pleasantly surprised.

Investigate

When we make big decisions in life, we do research. When we buy a house or a car, change jobs, or make an investment, we search online for comparable prices, check out what others say about it, and so on. The same should be true when looking at colleges. There are a million ways to research colleges, from the nuts and bolts on each college's website to talking to current students to reading books and magazines about the institution. Given the importance of the decision, it's impossible to do too much research on a college, and this hard work will pay off when your child is successful in choosing a good fit.

One of the most important ways to investigate a college and narrow down a college list is to visit the campus. A college visit isn't a drive-through on a weekend or even a stroll on the sidewalks. A college visit means taking every opportunity to fully experience life on campus. Just about every college offers visits at convenient times throughout the year, and they can be scheduled online or by calling the admissions office. There may be options when it comes to the visit and every opportunity should be taken. If they're not offered, ask.

These components of a college visit help kids immerse themselves in the culture, get the feel for the college, and help them determine if a college is right for them:

- *The official campus tour.* The tour is the quintessential part of the college visit. The tour takes teens and families to all corners of the campus, from the football field to the classroom, and from the biology labs to the library. Some parts of the tour might be optional but worth the extra time. Ask to see what a lecture room looks like, where the art studio is, and how to find the tutoring center. Those tour guides want to answer questions. It's the perfect time to ask all about life on campus from a kid's perspective. How did they choose this college? How many students stick around on weekends? What are their favorite and least favorite parts of the college?
- *Meetings with admissions staff.* What better way is there to find out more about the college than directly from the experts? The admissions staff can talk to your teen about what the first year of classes will look like, highlight available scholarships, and give hints on getting into the best dorm. In addition to admissions staff, you and your teen may also want to meet with others on campus, including coaches, faculty, or the financial aid office. Normally the admissions staff can set up these appointments for you.
- *Dining hall test drive.* A lot of people skip this step on their tour, but if they are going to be eating three square meals a day in one place, it's worth checking out. Many times the admissions staff will cover the cost of lunch for a prospective student and family, and if not, it's worth the price. Although a dining hall shouldn't be the final decision maker, it offers an impression that can help to seal the deal
- *Prospective student weekend.* Some colleges roll out the red carpet for high school juniors and seniors, inviting them to campus for a full day or even overnight. These prospective student weekends can help teens see what

life on campus is like by having them attend a class, interact with students, and sometimes even stay overnight in on-campus housing. These weekends can be few and far between, though, so check with prospective colleges early to get on the invite list.

Finalize the List

By the beginning of the senior year in high school, teens should have a fairly good idea of what colleges fit them best. Sometimes narrowing the list is an issue, but on the flip side, broadening the list can be tough for some kids. Many colleges and high school counselors recommend that kids apply to somewhere between three and five colleges. With the advent of the Common Application and other applications allowing them to apply to multiple schools at the same time, many teens now apply to even more.

A kid who has a good idea about what colleges fit him best—academically, geographically, culturally, and financially — should not need to apply to tens of colleges. Teens should narrow (or expand) their list to colleges that meet their needs and interests. And although they should own the list, it never hurts to bounce it off the school counselor or other trusted adult. Having a second unbiased set of eyes will help them talk through the whys of the list. School counselors or other experts can provide constructive feedback and ensure that kids are set up for success.

Applying to College

When the time comes to apply to college, the hard work has theoretically already been done. Applying to a purposeful set of colleges that fit is the primary goal throughout the college search process.

Plan Ahead

Senior year is a very busy time, and not everything on the college application needs to wait until then, so get an early start. By planning ahead, kids can alleviate the stress of the college application process and lighten the load in their senior year. Activities such as sending standardized test scores, requesting letters of recommendation, and writing college essays can all be completed ahead of the college application if the correct planning is done. Completing these steps before the start of senior year can save both time and money when it comes to applying to college.

When teens take a standardized test (e.g., ACT or SAT), they have the option to send their scores to a set number of colleges. Some choose to do this because it is included in their assessment fee. Others choose to wait and see what their score is or what their college list will look like and make the decision later. There are pros and cons to both options, but either way, test scores can be sent in the spring prior to the senior year as long as the kid's college list is fairly complete.

Many college applications require letters of recommendation, but some do not. Throughout the college search, it is good to keep this in mind and ask the college whether this will be a requirement for application. The letter of recommendation process varies from high school to high school, but many teachers appreciate being asked early to write a letter of recommendation. Seniors should choose teachers who know them well and can speak to how they learn, the value they bring to the classroom, and perhaps any challenges they have overcome. They should not choose teachers based strictly on the subject they teach. Aptitude will show on the transcript, so seniors should choose teachers who can speak to their personal side. They also should not ask more teachers for a recommendation than the number required by the college applications. Normally colleges ask for one or two letters. Teachers can get overwhelmed with requests for letters, and many colleges will not review letters beyond the number specified in their application guidelines, so it is best to stick to the number required.

As with letters of recommendation, not every college requires an essay, but many do. As teens build a purposeful college list, they should investigate the need for an essay. In the past, colleges have had specific prompts for their essays, but many are now moving toward a broader approach. Applicants can prepare by creating a personal statement in their junior year and ask colleges whether their prompts will change for the following year. The Common Application releases its essay prompts early in the calendar year, allowing teens to begin to prepare in their junior year. Students should take advantage of this opportunity to be prepared and to review with teachers and counselors before the end of the junior year.

Start Early

Colleges have various deadlines for applications, but starting early is a good idea no matter what the deadline. As soon as senior year begins, kids should connect with their school counselor or registrar's office to confirm the process needed for requesting letters of recommendation, transcripts, and forms such as fee waivers or early decision approvals. For colleges with hard deadlines, gathering all the information, crafting a thoughtful application, and submitting far ahead of the deadline will ensure that the college receives each piece of the application with plenty of time to spare. For colleges with rolling deadlines, submitting early may provide an advantage with financial aid, housing, and the time it takes to receive a decision.

Follow Up

It never hurts to follow up on college applications. Many institutions provide applicants with an online portal. Kids can keep their eye on the process and make sure that everything has been submitted (and received) for evaluation. Some of these online portals have taken the place of the "fat envelope" that colleges used to send with admission decisions, making them even more important. If applicants have questions about their college application or if there is an admissions representative with whom they have built a relationship, a quick check is appropriate.

Making the Decision

Once college acceptances begin rolling in, kids face another choice: where to attend. This decision can come down to a few factors, but revisiting the questions to determine fit are extremely helpful in this situation. After all the materials from each college have been received, including which colleges they have been admitted to, the school or department that they will be in, and financial aid awards, a series of questions can help seal the deal—for example:

- Do I see myself on this campus?
- Will I be successful at this school?

- What happens if I change my major? Are there other majors of interest at this institution?
- Can I afford this college?   .

Although these questions closely overlap the questions on fit that helped to build the list, a teen should think through these in their new context. For example, the financial award letter will include the actual out-of-pocket costs for attendance. With this information, a frank family conversation should take place to evaluate each institution. Only they can decide which question carries the most weight, but the fact that a purposeful list of colleges was built to begin with will make the decision much easier.

Making the Most of College

No matter where they end up, students can make the most of the college experience while they are there. Although it may seem like an eternity to an eighteen-year-old freshman, college goes by in the blink of an eye. But mistakes can be expensive and detrimental in so many ways. If kids come to college prepared to succeed, they can minimize these mistakes and maximize their productivity.

Give It a Chance

All too often, first-year students arrive on campus and find it tough to adjust to a new way of life. They have to make new friends, learn a new city, and adapt to roommate living. Everyone is in a new position, and it can get overwhelming for them. Encourage your kid to give college a chance and not give up on it right away. Teens who have a negative attitude from the start are less likely to give their first few weeks on campus a chance and end up leaving after a semester or a school year. By immersing themselves into campus life and coming in with a positive attitude, they can set themselves up for success.

Get Involved

College students spend most of their time at college outside classes. This leaves much more time on their hands than they are used to. Upon (or even prior to) arrival, they should check out the cocurricular options on campus. There are intramural, club, and organized sports opportunities; student associations and interest-related clubs; volunteer organizations; and sororities and fraternities on some campuses. When students get involved, they can feel ownership in the institution as well as expand their circle of friends and acquaintances.

Ask for Help

The jump from high school to college is more challenging for some than for others, both academically and interpersonally. First-year students should learn about the various supports on campus that can help them succeed in all aspects of college life. Encourage them to ask their professors on the first day about office hours, study sessions, and other supports. Have them seek out the tutoring center and attend an orientation before classes even start. Resources also exist on campus to help students with their mental and physical health, and they should not feel embarrassed to reach out when needed. Student health and counseling services typically offer counseling, group meetings, and health screenings. These services are usually included in the tuition and fees, so students should use them when needed.

Maximize Opportunities

Opportunities abound at every college. By maximizing opportunities, they can feel more connected to the college, their major, and the community. For example, visiting the career services and alumni centers early in their college career can help students build connections and understand more about their college major and potential career paths. These visits can also help them construct relationships that may be useful as they begin to apply for internships and even job opportunities.

Getting involved in organizations is great, but maximizing that opportunity by becoming a leader on campus, volunteering in the community, and participating in advocacy issues can help students expand their network off campus and prepare for life after college.

Students can also take advantage of academic opportunities that can help them get to know their academic team, learn more about their major, and even build their résumé. They should ask their professors and academic departments what opportunities exist to help with projects, papers, or research. Even in their first year, students can begin to build their profile on campus.

14

Is Community College a Better Place to Start?

We have discussed how to think about whether a four-year college degree is a good option for your child and some of the risks and rewards associated with paying a substantial amount of money for a degree and spending at least four years and possibly much more preparing for a career. Community college provides an alternative in cases where going directly for a four-year degree might not make sense. For some students, going directly to a four-year college may cause personal and academic challenges that could derail their success and leave them without a degree at all while still stuck paying off student loans. Others may earn their four-year degree but incur a large amount of debt relative to the typical incomes of people in their ultimate career field. For these students, community college could be a smarter strategy for achieving the typical four-year degree career pathway.

On the flip side, some students may have a clear vision of what they want to accomplish in their career, and they have found local community colleges that offer the necessary preparation to enter that field directly. Career fields such as nursing, medical technology, information technology, and physical therapy provide well-paying entry-level jobs in growing industries to students with associate degrees that can be earned at a community college.

For motivated and focused students with clear career goals, community college can be an excellent and affordable route to this type of employment. But community college will be a very different experience from a four-year college, and that comes with its own set of challenges that can leave students disappointed or underprepared for their ultimate career goal. In this chapter, we will help you and your child explore the potential benefits of attending community college and the potential downsides.

Upsides of Community College

Let's start with the upsides. One of the most obvious benefits of community college is the lower cost of tuition. Average annual tuition and fees for a public two-year college are around $3,500 compared to about $9,500 for public four-year colleges (in-state students).[1] The potential savings are dramatically higher when comparing community college tuition to that of private four-year colleges or out-of-state tuition at public four-year colleges. Two years at a community college will be much less likely to leave your child with crushing student debt. If she ultimately wants to get a four-year degree by transferring after two years at a community college, she could potentially save 30 percent or even much more on just the tuition part of the cost of her total education. The cost savings could go even higher if she lives at home while studying at a community college.

Community college can also provide a second chance at academics. If your child did not get serious about academic study until late in high school or struggled with grades until he received additional support services or changed schools, community college can provide a chance to fix grades and demonstrate that he can be counted on to continue taking his academic work seriously.

There are students who have gone from a community college into an Ivy League university. When four-year colleges evaluate potential students for admission, by far the most important requirement is that the student will be able to successfully handle the academic work. Students don't always mature or develop adequate study skills in time to give that confidence to the admissions office. Even if they have an SAT or ACT score that suggests their innate ability is higher than their grades, colleges know that doing well is as much a matter of self-discipline and hard work as it is a matter of talent. It is worth noting here that if your child will attend community college as part of a long-term four-year college plan, then he needs to do the work needed to perform well in his community college courses to ensure he can get admitted to the four-year college.

Course difficulty can vary widely by departments and institutions, but generally community college courses are less demanding than four-year college courses. Students need to show they are capable of getting good grades in order to give the four-year college enough confidence that they will thrive on campus.

Community colleges also provide a lot of flexibility. Most offer evening and weekend courses that provide greater scheduling flexibility. Many students at community colleges are adults or other nontraditional students who have children or have regular jobs outside class. These schedules can be helpful for students who need to work to help cover the cost of their education or have other options they want to explore at the same time. This flexibility can also be useful for students who are testing the waters on whether college is right for them. Perhaps they are not sure if they need a college degree yet or if they can handle the academic work and do not yet want to commit to a four-year degree pathway that requires a full-time commitment. They can work full time or part time earning money and still take a few courses to get their feet wet and see how it goes.

Another upside is a strong focus on employment. For students who are intent on finding employment quickly and would like to begin working without spending four more years in a classroom, there are many community college programs that are specifically geared to preparing students for employment in excellent careers that offer very competitive pay even compared to some careers that require a four-year degree. A lot of technology companies, in particular, prefer to hire people for certain technical jobs who have specific skills they need rather than requiring a four-year degree. There is also nothing to prevent your child from using her community college degree to get started in a technical field and later complete a more advanced degree if she wants to develop her career further. Here are some examples of fast-growing, well-paying careers that your child could enter through community college preparation:

- *Medical technology and imaging.* This includes jobs like being a diagnostic medical sonographer who uses sonogram technology to test patients and diagnose diseases in a lab environment.

- *Engineering technology*. Many manufacturing companies have jobs that require technical knowledge of advanced manufacturing systems and technologies, but in many cases, this practical expertise can be learned without a full four-year engineering degree.
- *Dental hygiene*. Dental hygienists can get licensed with an associate degree. Starting salaries for clinical positions are typically only a small amount lower than they would be for someone with a four-year degree.
- *Nursing*. Becoming a registered nurse requires passing the NCLEX certification exam but does not require a four-year nursing degree. Those with an associate degree can qualify.

Yet another benefit for some students at community colleges is smaller class sizes and more personal attention from professors. At many four-year colleges, a typical required course for freshmen is a weekly lecture that takes place in an auditorium with two hundred other students. The professor may be a charismatic lecturer, but it's unlikely any students will get much personal attention from her. The class will be divided among multiple teaching assistants who provide individual assistance to students who have questions. The knowledge, eagerness, and effectiveness of these teaching assistants may vary widely. This can be an intimidating experience for new college students, and it sometimes requires that students be more assertive and self-disciplined when they need extra help.

At a community college, the experience is usually much more intimate. Class sizes are more like what students experienced in high school, so professors can get to know students within the classroom and are more approachable outside class when someone needs to talk through a concept he doesn't quite understand. This kind of attention and intimacy can be helpful for students who may not be ready to jump into the deep end of a four-year college experience just yet and want a chance to get some of their standard requirements completed in a less stressful environment while they mature as students. As we discuss later, though, this can be a double-edged sword.

Along the same lines as smaller class size, community colleges may reduce exposure to high-risk behaviors and a drinking culture that exists on many four-year college campuses today. There are no fraternities, sororities, or extensive time periods for social interaction that students find on a four-year campus. Many community college students are career-focused adults and do not have time to participate in activities outside class. In addition, your child will most likely live at home while attending. If your child is anxious about coping with social pressure or intends to take a more aggressive course schedule to shorten the time spent meeting academic requirements, then community college could provide a better atmosphere in which to complete the first two years of a four-year degree. There can be a downside to this as well, depending on your child, which we discuss later in this chapter.

One benefit of community colleges that might not be readily apparent is the opportunity to try out a major with less at stake for those who change their minds. Many students end up changing their major while attending a four-year college. Both of us changed majors after completing some of the entry-level requirements in our initial course of study and had to scramble to make up credits in another major to graduate on time.

It is a common misconception that most students going off to a four-year college will graduate within four years. In fact, less than 20 percent of full-time students at many public universities earn their degree within four years. Only about 9 percent of public four-year universities graduate most of their students on time.[2] What this means in tangible terms for you as a parent is that there is a reasonable chance your child may need more than four years to graduate, and thus the cost of college may creep higher than you expected. By choosing to attend a community college for the first two years, the cost of making those changes can potentially be reduced, and it may take some pressure off your child to feel obligated to complete a certain major that she would otherwise prefer to change if it were not for the financial impact.

Finally, your child will be able to use money from her 529 college savings to attend community college. If you have been saving for college with a 529 plan, funds may be used for any community college tuition costs, just like they would be used at a four-year institution. There is a caveat for room and board expenses. In most cases, we are assuming if your child is attending community college, he will be living at home and will not incur room and board expenses. However, if he is enrolled at an institution less than part-time and still paying for some kind of room and board, those expenses will not be eligible for use of 529 funds.

Potential Downsides

Now let's turn to some of the potential downsides of attending community college. As you will see, some of the positive attributes of community college can also have a corresponding negative impact depending on the situation.

First, a large percentage of community college students are adults and nontraditional students rather than eighteen-year-old first-time students coming from high school and planning to earn a four-year degree. Community colleges are designed to support a wide range of local community member needs. Many of their students are working full-time jobs and have children. They may be attempting to return to college after many years in the workforce or may be trying to manage a quick career transition after losing a job that did not require a college education. There is nothing inherently wrong with this mission or these students, and community colleges are playing a critical role. But it can mean that your child may be surrounded by a lot of students in their classes who are less motivated, less prepared, and much less interested in a four-year degree than they are. One of the great benefits for eighteen-year-old freshmen attending a four-year college is that they are immediately immersed in a large group of peers with similar ambitions and a similar situation in life. That group can provide a lot of support and encouragement. Peers can be role models for success or help other freshmen through homesickness or show them a useful new way to study. Teens are more likely to feel that they are going it alone at a community college and may have fewer like-minded peers to turn to for inspiration, companionship, or help. For some students, this more "businesslike" feel of a community college can be appealing because they want to get it done and move on to a job as quickly as possible. For others, though, this could increase the risk that they lose steam and feel adrift, questioning whether college is right for them after all.

First-generation freshmen can be especially vulnerable to that feeling at a community college. Educational researchers have done studies that show that first-generation students are in fact more likely to graduate if they attend a more challenging four-year college because the expectations are higher and the peer group is more supportive. Everyone is riding the same wave so to speak. Think about whether your child has the self-discipline and internal drive to succeed and work through challenges more independently or whether she could benefit greatly from being immersed in a large group of supportive peers who can help carry her along to success.

One of the benefits we discussed was the fact that community college can be an easier academic transition for students because courses will be less difficult than at a four-year college on average. There can be a flip side to this, though, if your child's goal is to go on to attend a four-year college. Because the course work is not as rigorous at a community college, your child could still find herself in a situation where she is struggling to keep up and adjust academically once she transfers. By the time students take courses in their junior year of a four-year college, professors expect that they have developed strong study skills, can read multiple books every week, can produce well-written papers frequently, and can juggle multiple academically challenging classes at the same time. If community college was more like advanced high school for your child, she may have a tough adjustment period when transferring at the start of junior year. Your child might be surprised by how much more work she has to start doing in a four-year college, and this could lead her to question whether she is capable of persevering.

How much this would affect your child may depend on what she intends to study and where she is transferring. Similar to what we mentioned earlier, this issue can particularly affect first-generation students. Sometimes because these students lack confidence in their abilities, they chose to attend community college first, even when they were doing well academically in high school or have test scores that show they are capable of the work at a four-year college. They may believe that starting at a community college will make it easier for them to succeed, but research has shown that these students are more likely to succeed academically and graduate with a four-year degree if they go directly to the more challenging four-year college first. If your child is getting excellent grades in high school and demonstrating consistent self-discipline, don't be afraid to challenge her academic insecurities if she is leaning toward a community college simply because she lacks confidence rather than ability.

Another potential downside to community college is the temptation for some students to opt out of a more ambitious educational plan and go for a quicker path to a job so they can get out of the classroom and start earning money. Community college offers faster options for entering the workforce, but often with lower pay or a more career-limiting skill set than a four-year degree. We are not suggesting that students should aim for the maximum possible time in school before entering a career or that a student would be some kind of failure for choosing to be a nurse instead of an oncologist. We just want to point out that it is worth giving some thought to your child's goals and personality and thinking about whether she would be happier in the long run by committing to a more challenging four-year-degree career plan or is mature enough to avoid giving up too soon because of impatience or having an easy out. Community college is more like the roller coaster with a "chicken exit" at the front of the line. Some kids might be better off getting into a line where there is no chicken exit and being inspired and challenged to succeed at a bigger goal. Others may be relieved to know that they don't need to go down that four-year degree path to find happiness in life and start a good career and will appreciate the flexibility and more direct job pathways offered by a community college.

Community colleges do a great job of providing a wide range of foundational courses and then very specialized courses with a career-placement focus. But students who are on a four-year-degree path could miss out on some truly inspiring education. During our freshman and sophomore years at a large research university, we heard lectures by Carl Sagan, Kurt Vonnegut, and other world-renowned thinkers. We took history and psychology courses from professors who were famous for their insightful and engaging lectures. On any given day, there were forums, lectures, workshops, or seminars on everything from Chinese literature to nanotechnology. Many times we took courses from professors who wrote the most important books in their field, the same books that community college professors would use to teach that subject. The language department offered not only Spanish, German, and Chinese but also languages like Tagalog and Urdu. Those who wanted to study architecture in Italy could take a semester-abroad program there. And those interested in studying politics in Washington, DC, could take a semester program in DC. Even if we had teaching assistants instead of the professor helping with our physics classes, those assistants were doing cutting-edge research in their field and had access to world-class facilities. They were creating new knowledge in science, not just regurgitating what scientists already know.

It is hard to say how much that experience enriched our lives financially, but it absolutely enriched our lives intellectually and opened our minds to beautiful knowledge that inspired in us a lifelong love of learning, perhaps the greatest career skill of all. Whether this is worth something for your child is a deeply personal decision. It may seem like a luxury, but do not underestimate the power of a great four-year college to inspire young minds toward a life bigger than they had originally imagined for themselves. And keep in mind that many of these top colleges offer substantial financial aid to students with high potential who come from a low-income family.

We admit that we are personally disheartened by the trend these days to reduce college to an equation of money in and career out. It can be and should be much more than that. College can change lives. As you and your child consider the standard equation that cannot be ignored, try to spend some time discussing the bigger picture. Think about whether your child needs an extra dose of inspiration and could get it from the types of four-year colleges that will admit her.

A community college does not provide much in the way of campus life or the social and emotional development opportunities from a group experience. It is true that students can still experience this once they transfer into a four-year college as a junior, but they will miss out on some formative experiences that are more typical in a college dormitory environment. As we discussed previously, some parents and their kids may view this as positive. It is true that there are four-year colleges with campus cultures that encourage excessive drinking and partying, although at any institution, this will depend heavily on the social circles in which your child chooses to associate.

In fact, the social experience at a four-year college can be much more than parties. Four-year colleges often offer activities such as a multiday camping trip for summer orientation before freshman year that provide healthy and safe ways for your child to connect with their peers and begin building lifelong friendships. Many four-year colleges offer unique dormitories for special interest groups such as students interested in environmental issues or women's studies, or for students who want to be with other students of the same race or gender. Dormitories on campus at a four-year college have resident advisors, and often professors, who live in the same dormitory and provide both supervision and mentorship. The random encounters in dormitory hallways, study halls, and campus cafeterias can expose your child to people from different socioeconomic backgrounds, ethnicities, and countries, and offer the opportunity to develop valuable social skills that will pay off in the workplace. A student's freshman and sophomore years in particular provide opportunities for this type of concentrated social interaction and friendship formation and help develop your child's sense of independence away from home. By the time students are juniors, they may start to break off into their established groups of friends and live off campus. Students who transfer in from community college during this time may find it a bit harder to establish those connections or break into existing groups if they do not easily form new friendships. The value of campus life during these formative freshman and sophomore years depends greatly on what a college offers, where it is located, and the unique personality and interests of your child. It is worth spending some time thinking through the lifelong personal benefits that may come from having those special social experiences and whether your child would want to miss out on them.

Finally, the last but perhaps most important potential downside of community colleges is the issue of credit transfer. If your child is planning to attend community college as part of a larger strategy to obtain a four-year degree, you and he must be very careful to research and verify what credits from the community college will transfer successfully to a four-year college. We wish that this were an easier task. Sometimes the admissions office at a four-year college will tell you that credits will transfer but the actual department that reviews those credits for acceptance will tell you otherwise. Even if the name of a course and the course syllabus exactly match the same course that is taught at the four-year college, the department at that four-year college may not feel that the rigor of the course at the community college is sufficient and that the courses are not equivalent. Ostensibly this is to prevent students from coming in underprepared for the next level of course work, so they would say this is for your child's benefit. But if you have already paid tuition and your child has done the work, it can be hugely disappointing and also a financial burden. Some students have been forced to pause school and work until they can come up with the money to cover the additional cost of recompleting course work after they transferred. This is where it can very helpful to attend a community college with well-established credit transfer agreements with other public colleges in your area. In certain states, community colleges are required by law to have specific transfer agreements worked out ahead of time so that students can be confident that their credit will be accepted. But you should always personally verify that your child's specific course credit transfer assumptions are correct. It is best to verify with both the community college and the four-year college to which your child intends to transfer. This can get tricky if your child decides to change his intended major late in the game. He may have verified his original course plan but if he makes changes, he should go back and reverify his transfer plan. It never hurts to ask.

We hope this chapter has provided a lot for you and your child to discuss if you are considering community college as an option. We hope that we have also armed you with information that you can use to conduct more research about any community college your child is considering so that she can make a smarter decision. Although the cost of community college is lower and there may be only one or two choices available in your local area, programs within community colleges can vary widely and it's important that your child do as much research as she would when considering a four-year college and think through all of the potential advantages or disadvantages.

15

Closing Thoughts

We hope this book has provided some useful guidance and starting points for having important conversations with your child about their career, education and life goals. We have covered a lot of ground and it may feel over-whelming. Below is a quick summary of the most important points you can bring into your conversations with your child.

- There isn't a single "best" college or a "hot" career that will make or break your child's future. There are multiple colleges, careers, and pathways in life that fit your child's unique personality, strengths, interests, and needs.
- Has your child defined "success" for themselves? It's important for your child to reflect honestly on what they want out of work. Do they want a certain kind of day to day experience? Do they want to impact the world in a certain way? Do they want a certain amount of money to fund a specific lifestyle? Help them check these reflections against reality.
- Think about college and career at the same time. The strategy of getting into the "best college possible" and assuming that the career part will just work itself out is naïve and could end up wasting money and time. A

traditional college degree may not be the right direction for certain career goals.

- Every career field has certain stereotypes and the most popular career fields are often glamorized in the media or portrayed incorrectly on television. Every career comes with certain realities and the only way to get a true sense of them is to get out there and talk to real people in the field or experience it directly through an internship or job shadow. Encourage your child to take these steps before they commit to an expensive course of study.

- Your child can build more long-term career security by combining direct skills (engineering, coding, accounting) with "superskills" (communication, persuasion, learning, leadership).

- Statistically speaking, a college degree *on average* will lead to greater career and financial stability. However, these averages hide extreme differences depending on your child's aptitude for school, their career goals, their financial situation and the cost and quality of the college they might attend. Do your research! There are literally thousands of post-secondary educational options in the United States alone, and they are not all created equal. Use our suggestions for research starting points and consider alternative strategies such as two-year to bachelor's degree transitions.

- Your child should not be discouraged if they cannot seem to find a "passion". It may be that the best advice for your child is to go out there and just become good at something. There is a popular idea in our culture that success comes from following a passion or that we just need to find the thing that interests us the most and we will be all set. We have learned over the course of our lives, though, that sometimes passion can come from success. When you discover that you can do something well and be successful at it, that can inspire passion and bring personal joy. Be useful to the world, and it's pretty likely the world will give something good back to you.

Thank you for allowing us to share what we've learned, and thank you for taking the time to consider the critical issues your teenager is facing when choosing among various options for college and career. We wish you and your child the best of luck!

Additional Resources

In this section, we've compiled a list of some helpful websites, books, and articles that you and your child can use to apply concepts in this book or to do additional research.

Career Assessments

CareerKey
http://www.careerkey.org
Career Key is an interest assessment based on John Holland's theory of career choice, referenced in chapter 2. It uses your child's interests to recommend college majors and careers. Career Key is widely used in schools and is also available for purchase by individuals.

Gallup StrengthsExplorer
https://www.strengths-explorer.com
Gallup StrengthsExplorer, referenced in chapter 2, is a strengths assessment designed for children between the ages of 10 and 14. StrengthsExplorer is widely used in schools and is also available for purchase by individuals.

O*NET Interest Profiler
https://www.mynextmove.org/explore/ip
The U.S. Department of Labor provides free online access to the O*NET Interest Profiler, referenced in chapter 2, at the MyNextMove website.

Strengths for Success
https://www.humanesources.com/strengths-for-success
Strengths for Success is an online resource available for purchase by
individuals that helps you and your child to assess personality type as
well as work and learning preferences. It provides a detailed report that can
be helpful in identifying potential careers.

Academic Resources

Khan Academy
http://www.khanacademy.org
Khan Academy, referenced in chapter 4, is a vast source of free high-quality
education videos from elementary school–level all the way through
advanced college-level courses. This site can be particularly helpful if
your child is in middle school or high school and is struggling with some
specific academic concepts.

Barbara Oakley. *A Mind for Numbers: How to Excel at Math and Science.* New
York: Penguin, 2014. An excellent primer on how to learn math and
science and a hopeful book for anyone struggling with these topics.

Financial Aid Resources

FAFSA
https://fafsa.ed.gov
The Free Application for Federal Student Aid, referenced in chapter 12, is a
form that every family should submit during the senior year of high school.
Once the FAFSA has been submitted to colleges, they can make a
determination of the amount of loans, grants, and even scholarship money
they are able to offer. This website contains more information about the
FAFSA, as well as the application tool.

FAFSA4caster
https://fafsa.ed.gov/FAFSA/app/f4cForm
The FAFSA4caster, referenced in chapter 12, allows families to get a sneak peek
at the money they may be eligible for through the FAFSA. It uses tax and other
family financial information to simulate the outcome of FAFSA eligibility.

Federal Student Aid

https://studentaid.ed.gov/sa

The website of the Federal Student Aid office provides information about subsidized loans, unsubsidized loans, and grants, along with the many other resources to pay for college are covered in detail at this website. The website shows interest rates and payback requirements for loans.

CSS PROFILE

https://css.collegeboard.org

This tool, referenced in chapter 12, is used for additional financial aid and scholarship consideration by approximately 400 colleges, universities, and scholarship programs. The PROFILE website explains the details of the tool and provides the application and options to submit and pay for the PROFILE.

Today's Military

http://todaysmilitary.com

Today's Military, provided by the U.S. Department of Defense, is a comprehensive look at all of the military options available to students. It provides more details on some of the items covered in chapter 12, including enlistment, ROTC, and military academies and colleges. This website provides step-by-step instructions and links to information on testing, talking with a recruiter, and benefits of each opportunity.

Advanced Placement

https://apstudent.collegeboard.org

Advanced Placement courses are offered at thousands of high schools all over the world. The College Board's AP website explains each of the courses available and provides more information on sending AP scores to colleges and universities.

CLEP

https://clep.collegeboard.org

Many colleges accept CLEP test scores, referenced in chapter 12, for academic credit. The CLEP website provides information on the tests available, colleges that accept CLEP for credit, and registration and test site information.

Carol Stack and Ruth Vedvik. *Financial Aid Handbook: Getting the Education You Want for the Price You Can Afford.* Franklin Lakes, NJ: The Career Press, Inc., 2011.

College Search and Application Resources

Naviance
https://www.naviance.com
Naviance is an online college and career readiness resource used by nearly 12,000 elementary, middle, and high schools. It's available free to students and families, and includes many resources relevant to the topics in this book, including the O*NET Interest Profiler, Gallup StrengthsExplorer, and detailed profiles of every accredited U.S. college and university. Ask your school counselor if Naviance is available to your child.

BigFuture
https://bigfuture.collegeboard.org
BigFuture is a free website from the College Board—the organization that administers the SAT—with extensive resources for students and parents that help you search for colleges, majors, financial aid, and careers.

ACT
http://actstudent.org
The ACT is an assessment taken by many students to be used throughout the college admission process. This website provides information on the subjects in the exam, as well as registration and scoring information. This site also allows student to send their exam scores to additional institutions.

SAT
https://sat.collegeboard.org
The SAT is also an assessment used by colleges through the application process. This website provides more information on registration and the option to send scores to additional colleges. This site also includes a breakdown on the subjects in the exam as well as scoring procedures.

Common Application
http://commonapp.org
The Common Application allows students to send a single application to more than 700 colleges and universities. The Common Application also incorporates online teacher recommendations, counselor recommendations, and transcript delivery to provide a seamless experience for students and high schools.

Notes

Chapter 2

1. Retrieved from: https://careertech.org/career-clusters.
2. Shane J. Lopez, PhD. Clifton Youth *StrengthsExplorer*™ *Technical Report: Development and Initial Validation.* The Gallup Organization, February 2007, pp 6-7.
3. The Gallup Organization. *Are You Afraid of Your Weaknesses?* February 19, 2001. Retrieved from http://www.gallup.com/businessjournal/559/afraid-your-weaknesses.aspx.
4. Jack Zenger and Joe Folkman. *Key Insights from the Extraordinary Leader: 20 New Ideas about Leadership Development* p. 5. Retrieved from http://zengerfolkman.com/wp-content/uploads/2013/03/Extraordinary-Leader-Insights-Excerpts-from-The-Extraordinary-Leader.pdf.
5. Ibid.
6. Ibid. p. 4.
7. Lada Adamic and Onur Ismail Filiz. *Do Jobs Run in Families?* March 17, 2016. Retrieved from https://research.fb.com/do-jobs-run-in-families/.

Chapter 3

1. Anthony P. Carnevale, Nicole Smith, Michelle Melton, and Eric W. Price. *Learning While Earning: The New Normal.* Georgetown Center for Education and the Workforce, October 2015. Retrieved from https://cew.georgetown.edu/cew-reports/workinglearners/.

2. American Consumer Credit Counseling. *What Does It Cost to Support Adult Children or Elderly Parents?* Retrieved from http://talkingcents.consumercredit.com/2014/08/21/poll-results-infographic-what-does-it-cost-to-support-adult-children-or-elderly-parents/.
3. *State of the American Workplace.* The Gallup Organization, 2017, p. 19.

Chapter 4

1. Anthony P. Carnevale, Nicole Smith, and Michelle Melton. *STEM.* Georgetown University Center on Education and the Workforce, 2011. p. 42.

Chapter 5

1. Goldie Blumenstyk. "Liberal Arts Majors Have Plenty of Job Prospects, if They Have Some Specific Skills, Too." *The Chronicle of Higher Education.* June 9, 2016. Retrieved from http://www.chronicle.com/article/Liberal-Arts-Majors-Have/236749.
2. Debra Humphreys and Patrick Kelly. *How Liberal Arts and Sciences Majors Fare in Employment: A Report on Earnings and Long-Term Career Paths.* Association of American Colleges and Universities, 2014, p. 10.
3. Ibid. p. 7.

Chapter 8

1. Retrieved from https://www.glassdoor.com/Salary/DreamWorks-Animation-Salaries-E36343.htm.
2. Billboard Staff, "How Much Do Artists Make?: A Comprehensive Look—from Cover Bands to Mariah's Vegas Residency," *Billboard Magazine*, June 19, 2015. Retrieved from http://www.billboard.com/articles/business/6605326/how-much-do-artists-make-music-industry-earnings.

Chapter 10

1. Retrieved from http://borderzine.com/2013/03/college-students-tend-to-change-majors-when-they-find-the-one-they-really-love/.

Chapter 11

1. Edward B. Fiske, "Colleges' Tuition up 7 Percent to 8 Percent; Total Bill Can Exceed $16,000," *New York Times*, April 7, 1986. Retrieved from http://www.nytimes.com/1986/04/07/us/colleges-tuition-up-7-to-8-total-bill-can-exceed-16000.html.
2. Paul F. Campos, "The Real Reason College Tuition Costs So Much," *New York Times*, April 4, 2015. Retrieved from https://www.nytimes.com/2015/04/05/opinion/sunday/the-real-reason-college-tuition-costs-so-much.html.
3. Retrieved from https://cew.georgetown.edu/cew-reports/americas-divided-recovery/.
4. Retrieved from http://www.ted.com/talks/robert_waldinger_what_makes_a_good_life_lessons_from_the_longest_study_on_happiness.

Chapter 14

1. Retrieved from https://bigfuture.collegeboard.org/pay-for-college/college-costs/college-costs-faqs.
2. Retrieved from https://www.nytimes.com/2014/12/02/education/most-college-students-dont-earn-degree-in-4-years-study-finds.html.

Index